I0476833

U.S. Department of Justice
Office of Justice Programs
National Institute of Justice

National Institute of Justice

Law Enforcement and Corrections Standards and Testing Program

Guide for the Selection of
Chemical Agent and Toxic Industrial Material
Detection Equipment for Emergency First Responders

NIJ Guide 100-00

Volume I
June 2000

ABOUT THE LAW ENFORCEMENT AND CORRECTIONS STANDARDS AND TESTING PROGRAM

The Law Enforcement and Corrections Standards and Testing Program is sponsored by the Office of Science and Technology of the National Institute of Justice (NIJ), U.S. Department of Justice. The program responds to the mandate of the Justice System Improvement Act of 1979, which directed NIJ to encourage research and development to improve the criminal justice system and to disseminate the results to Federal, State, and local agencies.

The Law Enforcement and Corrections Standards and Testing Program is an applied research effort that determines the technological needs of justice system agencies, sets minimum performance standards for specific devices, tests commercially available equipment against those standards, and disseminates the standards and the test results to criminal justice agencies nationally and internationally.

The program operates through:

The *Law Enforcement and Corrections Technology Advisory Council* (LECTAC) consisting of nationally recognized criminal justice practitioners from Federal, State, and local agencies, which assesses technological needs and sets priorities for research programs and items to be evaluated and tested.

The *Office of Law Enforcement Standards* (OLES) at the National Institute of Standards and Technology, which develops voluntary national performance standards for compliance testing to ensure that individual items of equipment are suitable for use by criminal justice agencies. The standards are based upon laboratory testing and evaluation of representative samples of each item of equipment to determine the key attributes, develop test methods, and establish minimum performance requirements for each essential attribute. In addition to the highly technical standards, OLES also produces technical reports and user guidelines that explain in nontechnical terms the capabilities of available equipment.

The *National Law Enforcement and Corrections Technology Center (NLECTC),* operated by a grantee, which supervises a national compliance testing program conducted by independent laboratories. The standards developed by OLES serve as performance benchmarks against which commercial equipment is measured. The facilities, personnel, and testing capabilities of the independent laboratories are evaluated by OLES prior to testing each item of equipment, and OLES helps the NLECTC staff review and analyze data. Test results are published in Equipment Performance Reports designed to help justice system procurement officials make informed purchasing decisions.

Publications are available at no charge through the National Law Enforcement and Corrections Technology Center. Some documents are also available online through the Internet/World Wide Web. To request a document or additional information, call 800-248-2742 or 301-519-5060, or write:

National Law Enforcement and Corrections Technology Center
P.O. Box 1160
Rockville, MD 20849-1160
E-Mail: *asknlectc@nlectc.org*
World Wide Web address: *http://www.nlectc.org*

The National Institute of Justice is a component of the Office of Justice Programs, which also includes the Bureau of Justice Assistance, Bureau of Justice Statistics, Office of Juvenile Justice and Delinquency Prevention, and the Office for Victims of Crime.

U.S. Department of Justice
Office of Justice Programs
National Institute of Justice

Guide for the Selection of Chemical Agent and Toxic Industrial Material Detection Equipment for Emergency First Responders

NIJ Guide 100-00

Dr. Alim A. Fatah[1]

John A. Barrett[2]
Richard D. Arcilesi, Jr.[2]
Dr. Kenneth J. Ewing[2]
Charlotte H. Lattin[2]
Michael S. Helinski[2]

Coordination by
Office of Law Enforcement Standards
National Institute of Standards and Technology
Gaithersburg, MD 20899

Prepared for
National Institute of Justice
Office of Science and Technology
Washington, DC 20531

June 2000

NCJ184449

This document was prepared under CBIAC contract number SPO-900-94-D-0002 and in coordination with Interagency Agreement M92361 between NIST and the Department of Defense Technical Information Center.

[1]National Institute of Standards and Technology, Office of Law Enforcement Standards
[2]Battelle Memorial Institute

National Institute of Justice

Julie E. Samuels
Acting Director

The technical effort to develop this guide was conducted
under Interagency Agreement 94-IJ-R-004,
Project No. 99-060-CBW.

This guide was prepared by the Office of Law Enforcement
Standards (OLES) of the National Institute of Standards
and Technology (NIST) under the direction of
Alim A. Fatah, Program Manager for
Chemical Systems and Materials, and
Kathleen M. Higgins, Director of OLES.

The work resulting from this guide was
sponsored by the National Institute of Justice (NIJ),
David G. Boyd, Director,
Office of Science and Technology.

Foreword

The Office of Law Enforcement Standards (OLES) of the National Institute of Standards and Technology (NIST) furnishes technical support to the National Institute of Justice (NIJ) program to support law enforcement and criminal justice in the United States. OLES's function is to develop standards and conduct research that will assist law enforcement and criminal justice agencies in the selection and procurement of quality equipment.

OLES is: (1) subjecting existing equipment to laboratory testing and evaluation, and (2) conducting research leading to the development of several series of documents, including national standards, user guides, and technical reports.

This document covers research conducted by OLES under the sponsorship of the NIJ. Additional reports as well as other documents are being issued under the OLES program in the areas of protective clothing and equipment, communications systems, emergency equipment, investigative aids, security systems, vehicles, weapons, and analytical techniques and standard reference materials used by the forensic community.

Technical comments and suggestions concerning this report are invited from all interested parties. They may be addressed to the Office of Law Enforcement Standards, National Institute of Standards and Technology, 100 Bureau Drive, Stop 8102, Gaithersburg, MD 20899-8102.

David G. Boyd, Director
Office of Science and Technology
National Institute of Justice

Acknowledgments

The authors wish to thank Ms. Kathleen Higgins of the National Institute of Standards and Technology (NIST) for programmatic support and for numerous valuable discussions concerning the contents of this document. Mr. Bill Haskell of SBCCOM, Mr. Richard Vigus of SBCCOM, Ms. Priscilla S. Golden of General Physics, and Mr. Todd Brethauer representing the Technical Support Working Group (TSWG) also reviewed the document and provided numerous useful comments.

We wish to acknowledge the Interagency Board (IAB) for Equipment Standardization and Interoperability. The IAB (made up of government and first responder representatives) was commissioned by the Attorney General of the United States in conjunction with the Department of Defense's Director of Military Support. The IAB was established to ensure equipment standardization and interoperability and to oversee the research and development of advanced technologies to assist first responders at the state and local levels in establishing and maintaining a robust crisis and consequence management capability.[3]

We also sincerely thank all vendors who provided us with information about their products.

---

[3] The Marshall Convention, Standardized Weapons of Mass Destruction (WMD) Response Force Equipment and InterOperability, 2 to 4 November 1999.

Contents

Tables

Figures

Commonly Used Symbols and Abbreviations

A	ampere	H	henry	nm	nanometer
ac	alternating current	h	hour	No.	number
AM	amplitude modulation	hf	high frequency	o.d.	outside diameter
cd	candela	Hz	hertz	Ω	ohm
cm	centimeter	i.d.	inside diameter	p.	page
CP	chemically pure	in	inch	Pa	pascal
c/s	cycle per second	IR	infrared	pe	probable error
d	day	J	joule	pp.	pages
dB	decibel	L	lambert	ppm	parts per million
dc	direct current	L	liter	qt	quart
°C	degree Celsius	lb	pound	rad	radian
°F	degree Fahrenheit	lbf	pound-force	rf	radio frequency
dia	diameter	lbf·in	pound-force inch	rh	relative humidity
emf	electromotive force	lm	lumen	s	second
eq	equation	ln	logarithm (base e)	SD	standard deviation
F	farad	log	logarithm (base 10)	sec.	Section
fc	footcandle	M	molar	SWR	standing wave ratio
fig.	Figure	m	meter	uhf	ultrahigh frequency
FM	frequency modulation	min	minute	UV	ultraviolet
ft	foot	mm	millimeter	V	volt
ft/s	foot per second	mph	miles per hour	vhf	very high frequency
g	acceleration	m/s	meter per second	W	watt
g	gram	N	newton	λ	wavelength
gr	grain	N·m	newton meter	wt	weight

area=unit^2 (e.g., ft^2, in^2, etc.); volume=unit^3 (e.g., ft^3, m^3, etc.)

ACRONYMS SPECIFIC TO THIS DOCUMENT

BAW	Bulk Acoustic Wave	IMS	Ion Mobility Spectrometry
CA	Chemical Agent	LIDAR	Light Detection and Ranging
CZE	Capillary Zone Electrophoresis	LCt$_{50}$	(Lethal Concentration x Time)$_{50}$
SF	Selection Factor	MS	Mass Spectrometry
FID	Flame Ionization Detector	NFPA	National Fire Protection Association
FLIR	Forward Looking Infrared	PCR	Polymerase Chain Reaction
FPD	Flame Photometric Detector	PID	Photo Ionization Detection
FTIR	Fourier Transform Infrared	SAT	Sensor Array Technology
GC	Gas Chromatography	SAW	Surface Acoustic Wave
HPLC	High Performance Liquid Chromatography	SCBA	Self Contained Breathing Apparatus
IC	Ion Chromatography	TICs	Toxic Industrial Chemicals
IDLH	Immediately Dangerous to Life and Health	TIMs	Toxic Industrial Materials
IR	Infrared		

PREFIXES
(See ASTM E380)

d	deci (10^{-1})	da	deka (10)
c	centi (10^{-2})	h	hecto (10^2)
m	milli (10^{-3})	k	kilo (10^3)
μ	micro (10^{-6})	M	mega (10^6)
n	nano (10^{-9})	G	giga (10^9)
p	pico (10^{-12})	T	tera (10^{12})

COMMON CONVERSIONS

0.30480 m =1ft	4.448222 N = lbf
2.54 cm = 1 in	1.355818 J =1 ft·lbf
0.4535924 kg = 1 lb	0.1129848 N m = lbf·in
0.06479891g = 1gr	14.59390 N/m =1 lbf/ft
0.9463529 L = 1 qt	6894.757 Pa = 1 lbf/in^2
3600000 J = 1 kW·hr	1.609344 km/h = mph

Temperature: $T^{\circ}_C = (T^{\circ}_F - 32) \times 5/9$ Temperature: $T^{\circ}_F = (T^{\circ}_C \times 9/5) + 32$

Executive Summary

The National Institute of Justice is the focal point for providing support to state and local law enforcement agencies in the development of counterterrorism technology and standards, including technological needs for chemical and biological defense. In recognizing the needs of state and local emergency first responders, the National Institute of Standards and Technology, working with the National Institute of Justice, the Technical Support Working Group, the U.S. Army Soldier and Biological Chemical Command, and the Interagency Board, is developing chemical and biological defense equipment guides. The guides will focus on chemical and biological equipment in areas of detection, personal protection, decontamination, medical, and communication. This document focuses specifically on chemical detection equipment for chemical agents and toxic industrial materials and was developed to assist the emergency first responder community in the evaluation and purchase of chemical detection equipment.

The long range plans are to: (1) subject existing chemical detection equipment to laboratory testing and evaluation against a specified protocol, and (2) conduct research leading to the development of a series of documents, including national standards, user guides, and technical reports. It is anticipated that the testing, evaluation, and research processes will take several years to complete; therefore, the National Institute of Justice has developed this initial guide for the emergency first responder community in order to facilitate their evaluation and purchase of chemical detection equipment.

In conjunction with this program, additional guides, as well as other documents, are being issued in the areas of biological agent detection equipment, decontamination equipment, personal protective equipment, medical kits and equipment, and communications equipment used in conjunction with protective clothing and respiratory equipment.

The information contained in this guide has been obtained through literature searches and market surveys. The vendors were contacted multiple times during the preparation of this guide to ensure data accuracy. In addition, the information is supplemented with test data obtained from other sources (e.g., Department of Defense) if available. It should also be noted that the purpose of this guide is not to provide recommendations but rather to serve as a means to provide information to the reader to compare and contrast commercially available detection equipment. *Reference herein to any specific commercial products, processes, or services by trade name, trademark, manufacturer, or otherwise does not necessarily constitute or imply its endorsement, recommendation, or favoring by the United States Government. The information and statements contained in this guide shall not be used for the purposes of advertising, nor to imply the endorsement or recommendation of the United States Government.*

With respect to information provided in this guide, neither the United States Government nor any of its employees make any warranty, expressed or implied, including but not limited to the warranties of merchantability and fitness for a particular purpose. Further, neither the United States Government nor any of its employees assume any legal liability or responsibility for the accuracy, completeness, or usefulness of any information, apparatus, product or process disclosed.

Technical comments, suggestions, and product updates are encouraged from interested parties. They may be addressed to the Office of Law Enforcement Standards, National Institute of Standards and Technology, 100 Bureau Drive, Stop 8102, Gaithersburg, MD 20899-8102. It is anticipated that this guide will be updated periodically.

Questions relating to the specific devices included in this document should be addressed directly to the proponent agencies or the equipment manufacturers. Contact information for each equipment item included in this guide can be found in Volume II.

GUIDE FOR THE SELECTION OF
CHEMICAL AGENT AND TOXIC INDUSTRIAL MATERIAL
DETECTION EQUIPMENT FOR
EMERGENCY FIRST RESPONDERS

This guide includes information intended to be useful to the emergency first responder community in the selection of chemical agent and toxic industrial material detection techniques and equipment for different applications. It includes a thorough market survey of chemical agent and toxic industrial material technologies and commercially available detectors known to the authors as of May 2000. Brief technical discussions are presented that consider the principles of operation of the various technologies. These may be ignored by readers who find them too technical, while those wanting additional technical information can obtain it from the extensive list of references that is included in Appendix B.

SECTION 1.0
INTRODUCTION

The primary purpose of this guide is to provide emergency first responders with information to aid them in the selection and utilization of chemical agent (CA) and toxic industrial material (TIM) detection equipment. The guide is more practical than technical and provides information on a variety of factors that can be considered when purchasing detection equipment, including sensitivity, detection states, and portability to name a few.

Due to the large number of chemical detection equipment items identified in this guide, the guide is separated into two volumes. Volume I represents the actual guide and Volume II serves as a supplement to Volume I since it contains the detection equipment data sheets only.

This guide contains information that should aid emergency first responders in the selection and utilization of chemical agent and TIM detection equipment. Some technical information is included in sections describing how the various detection technologies work. Readers finding this material too technical can omit this information while still making use of the rest of the guide, and readers desiring more technical detail can obtain it from the references listed in Appendix B and the data sheets provided in Volume II. The remainder of this guide (i.e., Volume I) is divided into five sections. Section 2.0 provides an introduction to chemical agents and TIMs. Specifically, it discusses nerve and blister agents by providing overviews, physical and chemical properties, routes of entry, and symptoms. It also discusses the 98 TIMs that are considered in this guide. Section 3.0 presents an overview of the identified chemical agent and TIM detection technologies. For each technology, a short description is provided along with photographs of specific equipment that falls within the technology discussed. Section 4.0 discusses various characteristics and performance parameters that are used to evaluate chemical agent and TIM detection equipment in this guide. These characteristics and performance parameters are referred to as selection factors in the remainder of this guide. Sixteen selection factors have been identified. These factors were compiled by a panel of experienced scientists and engineers with multiple years of experience in chemical agent and TIM detection and analysis, domestic preparedness, and identification of emergency first responder needs. The factors have also been shared with the emergency first responder community in order to get their thoughts and comments. Section 5.0 presents several tables that allow the reader to compare and contrast the different detection equipment utilizing the 16 selection factors.

Two appendices are also included within this guide. Appendix A lists questions that could assist emergency first responders selecting detection equipment. Appendix B lists the documents that were referenced in the guide.

SECTION 2.0
INTRODUCTION TO CHEMICAL AGENTS AND
TOXIC INDUSTRIAL MATERIALS

The purpose of this section is to provide a description of chemical agents (CAs) and toxic industrial materials (TIMs). Section 2.1 provides the discussion of chemical agents and section 2.2 provides the discussion of TIMs.

2.1   Chemical Agents

Chemical agents are chemical substances that are intended for use in warfare or terrorist activities to kill, seriously injure, or seriously incapacitate people through their physiological effects. A chemical agent attacks the organs of the human body in such a way that it prevents those organs from functioning normally. The results are usually disabling or even fatal.

The most common chemical agents are the nerve agents, GA (Tabun), GB (Sarin), GD (Soman), GF, and VX; the blister agents, HD (sulfur mustard) and HN (nitrogen mustard); and the arsenical vesicants, L (Lewisite). Other toxic chemicals such as hydrogen cyanide (characterized as a chemical blood agent by the military) are included as TIMs under Section 2.2 of this guide.

2.1.1   Nerve Agents

This section provides an overview of nerve agents. A discussion of their physical and chemical properties, their routes of entry, and descriptions of symptoms is also provided.

2.1.1.1   Overview

Among lethal chemical agents, the nerve agents have had an entirely dominant role since World War II. Nerve agents acquired their name because they affect the transmission of impulses in the nervous system. All nerve agents belong to the chemical group of organo-phosphorus compounds; many common herbicides and pesticides also belong to this chemical group. Nerve agents are stable, easily dispersed, highly toxic, and have rapid effects when absorbed both through the skin and the respiratory system. Nerve agents can be manufactured by means of fairly simple chemical techniques. The raw materials are inexpensive but some are subject to the controls of the Chemical Weapons Convention and the Australia Group Agreement.

2.1.1.2   Physical and Chemical Properties

The nerve agents considered in this guide are:

- GA: A low volatility persistent chemical agent that is taken up through skin contact and inhalation of the substance as a gas or aerosol. Volatility refers to a substance's ability to become a vapor at relatively low temperatures. A highly volatile (non-persistent) substance poses a greater respiratory hazard than a less volatile (persistent) substance.

- GB: A volatile non-persistent chemical agent mainly taken up through inhalation.
- GD: A moderately volatile chemical agent that can be taken up by inhalation or skin contact.
- GF: A low volatility persistent chemical agent that is taken up through skin contact and inhalation of the substance either as a gas or aerosol.
- VX: A low volatility persistent chemical agent that can remain on material, equipment, and terrain for long periods. Uptake is mainly through the skin but also through inhalation of the substance as a gas or aerosol.

Nerve agents in the pure state are colorless liquids. Their volatility varies widely. The consistency of VX may be likened to motor oil and is therefore classified as belonging to the group of persistent chemical agents. Its effect is mainly through direct contact with the skin. GB is at the opposite extreme; being an easily volatile liquid (comparable with, e.g., water), it is mainly taken up through the respiratory organs. The volatilities of GD, GA, and GF are between those of GB and VX. Table 2-1 lists the common nerve agents and some of their properties. Water is included in the table as a reference point for the nerve agents.

Table 2-1. Physical Properties of Common Nerve Agents

Property	GA	GB	GD	GF	VX	Water
Molecular weight	162.3	140.1	182.2	180.2	267.4	18
Density, g/cm^3*	1.073	1.089	1.022	1.120	1.008	1
Boiling-point, °F	464	316	388	462	568	212
Melting-point, °F	18	-69	-44	-22	< -60	32
Vapor pressure, mm Hg *	0.07	2.9	0.4	0.06	0.0007	23.756
Volatility, mg/m^3 *	610	22,000	3,900	600	10.5	23,010
Solubility in water, % *	10	Miscible with water	2	~2	Slightly	NA

* at 77 °F

2.1.1.3 Route of Entry

Nerve agents, either as a gas, aerosol, or liquid, enter the body through inhalation or through the skin. Poisoning may also occur through consumption of liquids or foods contaminated with nerve agents.

The route of entry also influences the symptoms developed and, to some extent, the sequence of the different symptoms. Generally, the poisoning works fastest when the agent is absorbed through the respiratory system rather than other routes because the lungs contain numerous blood vessels and the inhaled nerve agent can rapidly diffuse into the blood circulation and thus reach the target organs. Among these organs, the respiratory system is one of the most important. If a person is exposed to a high concentration of nerve agent, e.g., 200 mg sarin/m^3, death may occur within a couple of minutes.

The poisoning works slower when the agent is absorbed through the skin. Because nerve agents are somewhat fat-soluble, they can easily penetrate the outer layers of the skin, but it takes longer for the poison to reach the deeper blood vessels. Consequently, the first symptoms do not occur until 20 to 30 minutes after the initial exposure but subsequently, the poisoning process may be rapid if the total dose of nerve agent is high.

2.1.1.4 Symptoms

When exposed to a low dose of nerve agent, sufficient to cause minor poisoning, the victim experiences characteristic symptoms such as increased production of saliva, a runny nose, and a feeling of pressure on the chest. The pupil of the eye becomes contracted (miosis) which impairs night-vision. In addition, the capacity of the eye to change focal length is reduced and short-range vision deteriorates causing the victim to feel pain when trying to focus on nearby objects. This is accompanied by headache. Less specific symptoms are tiredness, slurred speech, hallucinations and nausea.

Exposure to a higher dose leads to more dramatic developments and symptoms are more pronounced. Bronchoconstriction and secretion of mucus in the respiratory system leads to difficulty in breathing and to coughing. Discomfort in the gastrointestinal tract may develop into cramping and vomiting, and there may be involuntary discharge of urine and defecation. There may be excessive salivating, tearing, and sweating. If the poisoning is moderate, typical symptoms affecting the skeletal muscles may be muscular weakness, local tremors, or convulsions.

When exposed to a high dose of nerve agent, the muscular symptoms are more pronounced and the victim may suffer convulsions and lose consciousness. The poisoning process may be so rapid that symptoms mentioned earlier may never have time to develop.

Nerve agents affect the respiratory muscles causing muscular paralysis. Nerve agents also affect the respiratory center of the central nervous system. The combination of these two effects is the direct cause of death. Consequently, death caused by nerve agents is similar to death by suffocation.

2.1.2 Blister Agents (Vesicants)

This section provides an overview of blister agents. A discussion of their physical and chemical properties, their routes of entry, and descriptions of symptoms is also provided.

2.1.2.1 Overview

There are two major families of blister agents (vesicants): sulfur mustard (HD) and nitrogen mustard (HN), and the arsenical vesicants (L). All blister agents are persistent and may be employed in the form of colorless gases and liquids. They burn and blister the skin or any other part of the body they contact. Blister agents are likely to be used to produce casualties rather than to kill, although exposure to such agents can be fatal.

2.1.2.2 Physical and Chemical Properties

In its pure state, mustard agent is colorless and almost odorless. It earned its name as a result of an early production method that resulted in an impure product with a mustard-like smell. Mustard agent is also claimed to have a characteristic odor similar to rotten onions. However, the sense of smell is dulled after only a few breaths so that the odor can no longer be distinguished. In addition, mustard agent can cause injury to the respiratory system in concentrations that are so low that the human sense of smell cannot distinguish them.

At room temperature, mustard agent is a liquid with low volatility and is very stable during storage. Mustard agent can easily be dissolved in most organic solvents but has negligible solubility in water. In aqueous solutions, mustard agent decomposes into non-poisonous products by means of hydrolysis but, since only dissolved mustard agent reacts, the decomposition proceeds very slowly. Oxidants such as chloramine (see page 24 for chloramine action), however, react violently with mustard agent, forming non-poisonous oxidation products. Consequently, these substances are used for the decontamination of mustard agent.

Arsenical vesicants are not as common or as stable as the sulfur or nitrogen mustards. All arsenical vesicants are colorless to brown liquids. They are more volatile than mustard and have fruity to geranium-like odors. These types of vesicants are much more dangerous as liquids than as vapors. Absorption of either vapor or liquid through the skin in adequate dosage may lead to systemic intoxication or death. The physical properties of the most common blister agents are listed in Table 2-2. Water is included in the table as a reference point for the blister agents.

Table 2-2. Physical Properties of Common Blister Agents

Property	HD	HN-1	HN-2	HN-3	L	Water
Molecular weight	159.1	170.1	156.1	204.5	207.4	18
Density, g/cm^3	1.27 at 68°F	1.09 at 77°F	1.15 at 68°F	1.24 at 77°F	1.89 at 68°F	1 at 77°F
Boiling-point, °F	421	381	167 at 15 mm Hg	493	374	212
Freezing-point, °F	58	-61.2	-85	-26.7	64.4 to 32.18	32
Vapor pressure, mm Hg	0.072 at 68°F	0.24 at 77°F	0.29 at 68°F	0.0109 at 77°F	0.394 at 68°F	23.756 at 77°F
Volatility, mg/m^3	610 at 68°F	1520 at 68°F	3580 at 77°F	121 at 77°F	4480 at 68°F	23,010 at 77°F
Solubility in water, %	<1%	Sparingly	Sparingly	Insoluble	Insoluble	NA

2.1.2.3 Route of Entry

Most blister agents are relatively persistent and are readily absorbed by all parts of the body. Poisoning may also occur through consumption of liquids or foods contaminated with blister agents. These agents cause inflammation, blisters, and general destruction of tissues. In the form of gas or liquid, mustard agent attacks the skin, eyes, lungs, and gastro-intestinal tract. Internal organs, mainly blood-generating organs, may also be injured as a result of mustard agent being taken up through the skin or lungs and transported into the body. Since mustard agent gives no immediate symptoms upon contact, a delay of between two and twenty-four hours may occur before pain is felt and the victim becomes aware of what has happened. By then, cell damage has already occurred. The delayed effect is a characteristic of mustard agent.

2.1.2.4 Symptoms

In general, vesicants can penetrate the skin by contact with either liquid or vapor. The latent period for the effects from mustard is usually several hours (the onset of symptoms from vapors is 4 to 6 hours and the onset of symptoms from skin exposure is 2 to 48 hours). There is no latent period for exposure to Lewisite.

Mild symptoms of mustard agent poisoning may include aching eyes with excessive tearing, inflammation of the skin, irritation of the mucous membranes, hoarseness, coughing and sneezing. Normally, these injuries do not require medical treatment.

Severe injuries that are incapacitating and require medical care may involve eye injuries with loss of sight, the formation of blisters on the skin, nausea, vomiting, and diarrhea together with severe difficulty in breathing. Severe damage to the eye may lead to the total loss of vision.

The most pronounced effects on inner organs are injury to the bone marrow, spleen, and lymphatic tissue. This may cause a drastic reduction in the number of white blood cells 5-10 days after exposure, a condition very similar to that after exposure to radiation. This reduction of the immune defense will complicate the already large risk of infection in people with severe skin and lung injuries.

The most common cause of death as a result of mustard agent poisoning is complications after lung injury caused by inhalation of mustard agent. Most of the chronic and late effects from mustard agent poisoning are also caused by lung injuries.

2.2 Toxic Industrial Materials

This section provides a general overview of TIMs as well as a list of the specific TIMs considered in this guide. Since the chemistry of TIMs is so varied, it is not feasible to discuss specific routes of entry and descriptions of symptoms.

Toxic industrial materials, or TIMs, are chemicals other than chemical warfare agents that have harmful effects on humans. TIMs, often referred to as toxic industrial chemicals, or TICs, are used in a variety of settings such as manufacturing facilities, maintenance areas, and general storage areas. While exposure to some of these chemicals may not be immediately dangerous to life and health (IDLH), these compounds may have extremely serious effects on an individual's health after multiple low-level exposures.

2.2.1 General

A TIM is a *specific type* of industrial chemical i.e., one that has a LCt_{50} value (lethal concentration for 50% of the population multiplied by exposure time) less than 100,000 mg-min/m^3 in any mammalian species and is produced in quantities exceeding 30 tons per year at one production facility. Although they are not as lethal as the highly toxic nerve agents, their ability to make a significant impact on the populace is assumed to be more related to the amount of chemical a terrorist can employ on the target(s) and less related to their lethality. None of these compounds are as highly toxic as the nerve agents, but they are produced in very large quantities (multi-ton) and are readily available; therefore, they pose a far greater threat than chemical agents. For instance, sulfuric acid is not as lethal as the nerve agents, but it is easier to disseminate large quantities of sulfuric acid because of the large amounts that are manufactured and transported every day. It is assumed that a balance is struck between the lethality of a material and the amount of materials produced worldwide. Materials such as the nerve agents are so lethal as to be in a special class of chemicals.

Because TIMs are less lethal than the highly toxic nerve agents, it is more difficult to determine how to rank their potential for use by a terrorist. Physical and chemical properties for TIMs such as ammonia, chlorine, cyanogen chloride, and hydrogen cyanide are presented in Table 2-3. Water is included in the table as a reference point for the TIMs. The physical and chemical properties for the remaining TIMs identified in this guide can be found in *International Task Force 25: Hazard From Industrial Chemicals Final Report*, April 1998. (See detailed reference in Appendix B).

Table 2-3. Physical and Chemical Properties of TIMs

Property	Ammonia	Chlorine	Cyanogen Chloride	Hydrogen Cyanide	Water
Molecular weight	17.03	70.9	61.48	27.02	18
Density, g/cm^3	0.00077 at 77°F	3.214 at 77°F	1.18 at 68°F	0.990 at 68°F	1 at 77°F
Boiling-point, °F	-28	-30	55	78	212
Freezing-point, °F	-108	-150	20	8	32
Vapor pressure, mm Hg at 77°F	7408	5643	1000	742	23.756
Volatility, mg/m^3	6,782,064 at 77°F	21,508,124 at 77°F	2,600,000 at 68°F	1,080,000 at 77°F	23,010 at 77°F
Solubility in water, %	89.9	1.5	Slightly	Highly soluble	NA

2.2.2 TIM Rankings

TIMs are ranked into one of three categories that indicate their relative importance and assist in hazard assessment. Table 2-4 lists the TIMs with respect to their Hazard Index Ranking (High, Medium, or Low Hazard).[2]

2.2.2.1 High Hazard

High Hazard indicates a widely produced, stored or transported TIM that has high toxicity and is easily vaporized.

2.2.2.2 Medium Hazard

Medium Hazard indicates a TIM that may rank high in some categories but lower in others such as number of producers, physical state, or toxicity.

2.2.2.3 Low Hazard

A Low Hazard overall ranking indicates that this TIM is not likely to be a hazard unless specific operational factors indicate otherwise.

---

[2] International Task Force 25: Hazard From Industrial Chemicals Final Report, April 1998.

Table 2-4. TIMs Listed By Hazard Index

High	Medium	Low
Ammonia	Acetone cyanohydrin	Allyl isothiocyanate
Arsine	Acrolein	Arsenic trichloride
Boron trichloride	Acrylonitrile	Bromine
Boron trifluoride	Allyl alcohol	Bromine chloride
Carbon disulfide	Allylamine	Bromine pentafluoride
Chlorine	Allyl chlorocarbonate	Bromine trifluoride
Diborane	Boron tribromide	Carbonyl fluoride
Ethylene oxide	Carbon monoxide	Chlorine pentafluoride
Fluorine	Carbonyl sulfide	Chlorine trifluoride
Formaldehyde	Chloroacetone	Chloroacetaldehyde
Hydrogen bromide	Chloroacetonitrile	Chloroacetyl chloride
Hydrogen chloride	Chlorosulfonic acid	Crotonaldehyde
Hydrogen cyanide	Diketene	Cyanogen chloride
Hydrogen fluoride	1,2-Dimethylhydrazine	Dimethyl sulfate
Hydrogen sulfide	Ethylene dibromide	Diphenylmethane-4,4'-diisocyanate
Nitric acid, fuming	Hydrogen selenide	Ethyl chloroformate
Phosgene	Methanesulfonyl chloride	Ethyl chlorothioformate
Phosphorus trichloride	Methyl bromide	Ethyl phosphonothioic dichloride
Sulfur dioxide	Methyl chloroformate	Ethyl phosphonic dichloride
Sulfuric acid	Methyl chlorosilane	Ethyleneimine
Tungsten hexafluoride	Methyl hydrazine	Hexachlorocyclopentadiene
	Methyl isocyanate	Hydrogen iodide
	Methyl mercaptan	Iron pentacarbonyl
	Nitrogen dioxide	Isobutyl chloroformate
	Phosphine	Isopropyl chloroformate
	Phosphorus oxychloride	Isopropyl isocyanate
	Phosphorus pentafluoride	n-Butyl chloroformate
	Selenium hexafluoride	n-Butyl isocyanate
	Silicon tetrafluoride	Nitric oxide
	Stibine	n-Propyl chloroformate
	Sulfur trioxide	Parathion
	Sulfuryl chloride	Perchloromethyl mercaptan
	Sulfuryl fluoride	sec-Butyl chloroformate
	Tellurium hexafluoride	tert-Butyl isocyanate
	n-Octyl mercaptan	Tetraethyl lead
	Titanium tetrachloride	Tetraethyl pyroposphate
	Trichloroacetyl chloride	Tetramethyl lead
	Trifluoroacetyl chloride	Toluene 2,4-diisocyanate
		Toluene 2,6-diisocyanate

SECTION 3.0
OVERVIEW OF CHEMICAL AGENT AND TIM DETECTION
TECHNOLOGIES

The applicability of chemical agent and TIM detection equipment to potential user groups will be dependent upon the characteristics of the detection equipment, as well as the type of chemical agent or TIM detected and the objective of the first responder unit. Numerous technologies are available for the detection of chemical agent and TIM vapors, some technologies are available for detection and identification of liquid droplets of chemical agents on surfaces, and many laboratory-based technologies exist for detection of TIMs in water. The quality of analytical results from the various analyzers is dependent upon the ability to effectively sample the environment and get the sample to the analyzer.

Analyzers designed for analysis of vapors will not be readily applicable for detection of low volatility liquid contamination on surfaces or contamination in water. Also, many analyzers could have difficulty in identifying a small amount of chemical agent or TIM in a high background of non-hazardous environmental chemicals. For example, a chemical vapor detector may readily detect trace levels of chemical agents or TIMs in an outdoor setting such as a forest or an open field, but the same detector may not be capable of detecting the same level of chemical agent or TIM in a crowded subway station or on a busy city street. These environments contain many chemicals produced by everyday activities (driving an automobile, using deodorant/perfumes, using insecticides, etc.) that look like a chemical agent or TIM to the analyzer and may affect the reliability of the instrument as well as its sensitivity. In this manner, the operator can become familiar with the peculiarities of the analyzer when exposed to various environmental chemicals expected in operational areas. As technological advances are made, more effective and accurate methods of detection that are less affected by environmental chemicals in operational areas will become commercially available at lower costs.

Chemical agents can be detected by several means that incorporate various technologies. The technologies are grouped into five major categories: point detection, stand-off detection, analytical instruments, sorbent sampling, and colormetric (color change). The type of technology needed for CA and TIM detection will be dependent on the type of CA agent or TIM used and the objective of the first responder unit.

3.1 Point Detection Technologies

Point detection technology is applicable in determining the type of chemical agent or TIM employed and can be used to map out contaminated areas if enough time is available. Point detectors can be used as warning devices to alert personnel to the presence of a toxic vapor cloud. In this scenario, the detector is placed up-wind of the first responder location. When the toxic chemical is carried towards this location, it first encounters the detector, thus sounding an alarm allowing the first responders to don the necessary protective clothing. It should be noted that if the concentration of chemical agent or TIM is high enough to be immediately life threatening, point detectors may not provide sufficient time to take protective measures. Another use of a point detector would be to monitor the vapor contamination originating from a decontamination site. Point detectors can also be used to determine which people have been contaminated, i.e., contamination triage. Contamination triage can be used to identify highly contaminated personnel, lightly contaminated personnel, and uncontaminated personnel with the idea that all contaminated people need rapid decontamination while non-contaminated people do not need to be decontaminated, thereby saving resources.

3.1.1 Ionization/Ion Mobility Spectrometry (IMS)

A detector using IMS technology is typically a stand-alone detector that samples the environment using an air pump. Contaminants in the sampled air are ionized and passed through a weak electric field toward an ion detector. The time it takes the species to traverse the distance is proportional to the mass of the ionized chemical species and is used as a means of identification. Analysis time ranges from several seconds to a few minutes.

Ionization of gaseous species can be achieved at atmospheric pressure. Using proton transfer reactions, charge transfer, dissociative charge transfer, or negative ion reactions such as ion transfer, nearly all chemical classes can be ionized. However, most IMS portable detectors use radioactive Beta emiters to ionize the sample.

IMS requires a vapor or gas sample for analysis; therefore, liquid samples must first be volatilized. The gaseous sample is drawn into a reaction chamber by a pump where a radioactive source, generally Ni^{63} (Nickel 63) or Am^{241} (Americium 241), ionizes the molecules present in the sample. The ionized air sample, including any ionized chemical agent, is then injected into a closed drift tube through a shutter that isolates the contents of the drift tube from the atmospheric air. The drift tube has a minor electrical charge gradient that draws the sample towards a receiving electrode at the end of the drift tube. Upon ion impact, an electrical charge is generated and recorded with respect to a travel time. The travel time is measured from the introduction gate to the receiving electrode.

The ions impact the electrode at different intervals providing a series of peaks and valleys in electrical charge that is usually graphed on Cartesian Coordinates. The Y-axis corresponds to the intensity of the charge received by impact of the various species that have respective travel times in the drift tube. This travel time in the drift tube and the strength of the charge gives a relative concentration of species in the sample.

An example of a handheld detector using this technology is the APD 2000, manufactured by Environmental Technologies Group, Incorporated. This detector is shown in Figure 3-1.

*Figure 3-1. APD 2000 Environmental
Technologies Group, Incorporated*

The M8A1 Automatic Chemical Agent Alarm System is another example of an IMS technology chemical agent detection and warning system. It incorporates the M43A1 detector to detect the presence of nerve agent vapors or inhalable aerosols. The M43A1 detector is an ionization product diffusion/ion mobility type detector. Air is continuously drawn through the internal sensor by a pump at a rate of approximately 1.2 L/min. Air and agent molecules are first drawn past a radioactive source (^{241}Am), and a small percentage are ionized by the beta rays. The air and agent ions are then drawn through the baffle sections of the cell. The lighter air ions diffuse to the walls and are neutralized more quickly than the heavier agent ions that have more momentum and are able to pass through the baffled section. As a result, the collector senses a greater ion current when nerve agents are present compared to the current when only clean air is sampled. An electronic module monitors the current produced by the sensor and triggers the alarm when a critical threshold of current is reached.

3.1.2 Flame Photometry

Flame photometry is based upon burning ambient air with hydrogen gas. The flame decomposes any chemical agents or TIMs present in the air. Compounds that contain phosphorus and sulfur produce hydrogen phosphorus oxygen (HPO) and elemental sulfur (S), respectively. At the elevated flame temperature, the phosphorus and sulfur emit light of specific wavelengths. A set of optimal filters is used to selectively transmit only the light emitted from the presence of phosphorus and sulfur to a photo-multiplier tube, which produces an analog signal related to the concentration of the phosphorus and sulfur containing compounds in the air. Since the classical nerve agents all contain phosphorus and sulfur and mustard contains sulfur, these agents are readily detected by flame photometry. Flame photometry is sensitive and allows ambient air to be sampled directly. However, it is also prone to false alarms from interferants that contain phosphorus and sulfur. The number of false positives due to interference can be minimized using algorithms. Using a flame photometric detector (FPD) in cooperation with a gas chromatograph will further reduce the likelihood of false alarms. There are a

15

number of gas chromatographs that use FPDs for detection purposes. Gas chromatographs are discussed in section 3.3.

3.1.3 Infrared Spectroscopy

Infrared spectroscopy is the measurement of the wavelength and intensity of the absorption of mid-infrared light by a sample. Mid-infrared light (2.5 – 50 μm, 4000 – 200 cm^{-1}) is energetic enough to excite molecular vibrations to higher energy levels. The wavelengths of IR absorption bands are characteristic of specific types of chemical bonds and every molecule has a unique IR spectrum (fingerprint). IR spectroscopy finds its greatest utility for identification of organic and organometallic molecules. There are two IR spectroscopy technologies employed in point detectors: photoacoustic infrared spectroscopy (PIRS) and filter based infrared spectroscopy. These two technologies and specific detector examples are discussed in the remainder of this section.

3.1.3.1 Photoacoustic Infrared Spectroscopy (PIRS)

Photoacoustic detectors use the photoacoustic effect to identify and detect chemical agent vapors. When a gas absorbs infrared radiation, its temperature rises and in turn causes the gas to expand. If the intensity of the infrared radiation is modulated, the sample will expand and contract. If the modulation frequency is an audible frequency, a microphone can be used to detect the resulting sound. Photoacoustic gas detectors use various filters to selectively transmit specific wavelengths of light that are absorbed by the chemical agent being monitored. The greater number of wavelengths used to identify the unknown, the fewer interferants will be observed. When no chemical agent is present in the atmospheric sample, the specific wavelength infrared light is typically not absorbed and, therefore, no audible signal is detected. When chemical agent is present in the sample, an audible signal (at the frequency of modulation) is produced by the absorption of the modulated infrared light. Selectivity can be increased by sequentially exposing the sample to several wavelengths of light. Chemical agents are distinguished from interferants by the relative signal produced when several different wavelengths are sequentially transmitted to the sample. Photoacoustic detectors are sensitive to external vibration and humidity. However, as long as the detector is calibrated in each operating environment immediately prior to sampling, selectivity will be very high. Innova produces two detectors that rely on photoacoustics. A mobile laboratory unit that utilizes the photoacoustic IR spectroscopy technology is the Innova Type 1301. A similar portable unit also manufactured by Innova is the Type 1312 detector. Both instruments are shown in Figures 3-2 and 3-3.

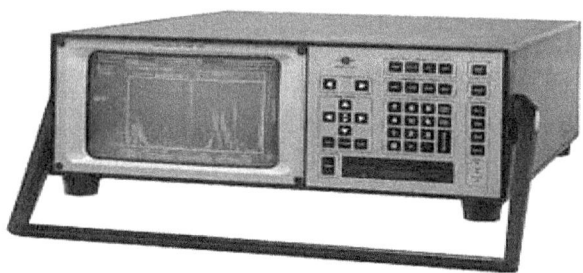

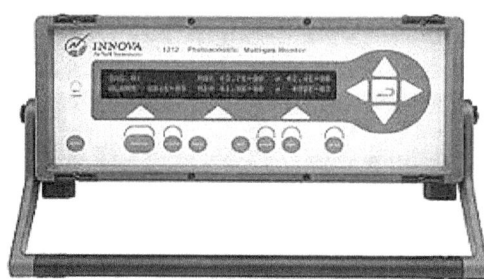

Figure 3-2. Innova Type 1301 Multigas Monitor   *Figure 3-3. Innova Type 1312 Multigas Monitor*

3.1.3.2 Filter Based Infrared Spectrometry

The filter based infrared spectrometry technology is based upon a series of lenses and mirrors that directs a narrow bandpass infrared beam in a preselected path through the sample. The amount of energy absorbed by the sample is measured and stored in memory. The same sample is examined at as many as four additional wavelengths. This multiwavelength, multicomponent data is analyzed by the microprocessor utilizing linear matrix algebra. Concentrations of each component, in each sample, at each station, are used for compiling time weighted average (TWA) reports and trend displays. The DMCS retains data for further analysis and longer term storage and retrieval. The Foxboro Company produces two of these detectors: (1) the Miran SaphIRe, a portable ambient air analyzer, and (2) the Miran 981B, a multipoint ambient air monitoring system. The Miran SaphIRe is shown in Figure 3-4.

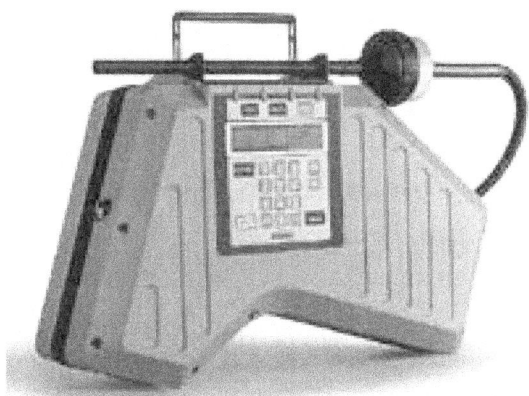

Figure 3-4. Miran SaphIRe Portable Ambient Air Analyzer

3.1.4 Electrochemistry

Electrochemical detectors monitor a change in electric potential of a solution or thin film when a chemical agent is absorbed. An example of one type of reaction is the inhibition of cholinesterase by nerve agents. A solution containing a known amount of cholinesterase is exposed to an air sample that may contain nerve agent. If nerve agent is present, a percentage of the cholinesterase will be inhibited from reaction in the next step. The next step involves adding a solution containing a compound that will react with uninhibited cholinesterase to produce an electrochemically active product. The resulting cell potential is related to the concentration of uninhibited cholinesterase, which is related to the concentration of nerve agent present in the sampled air. Another type of electrochemical detector monitors the resistance of a thin film that increases as the film absorbs chemical agent from the air. Electrochemical detectors are selective, however, they are not as sensitive as technologies such as IMS and flame photometry. Several of the fielded electrochemical detectors encounter problems when exposed to environmental extremes. Hot and cold temperatures change the rates of reactions and shift the equilibrium point of the various reactions, which affects sensitivity and selectivity.

3.1.5 Colorimetric or Color Change Chemistry

Detector kits, or tickets, are wet chemistry techniques formulated to indicate the presence or absence of a chemical agent by a color change resulting from a chemical reaction involving the suspect agent. These kits are usually used to verify the presence of a chemical agent after an alarm is received from another monitor. The kits are also used to test drinking water for contamination. A similar detection method using this technology is detection paper, which contains a dye that is colorless when crystalline and colored when dissolved in a chemical agent. Detector papers are generally used for testing suspect droplets or liquids on a surface. For gaseous or vaporous chemical agents, colorimetric tubes are also available. These consist of a glass tube that has the reacting compound sealed inside. Upon use, the tips of the tubes are broken off and a pump is used to draw the sample across the reacting compound (through the tube). If a chemical agent is present, a reaction resulting in a color change takes place in the tube. Draeger manufactures a number of colorimetric tubes. A picture of the Draeger colorimetric tubes is shown in Figure 3.5.

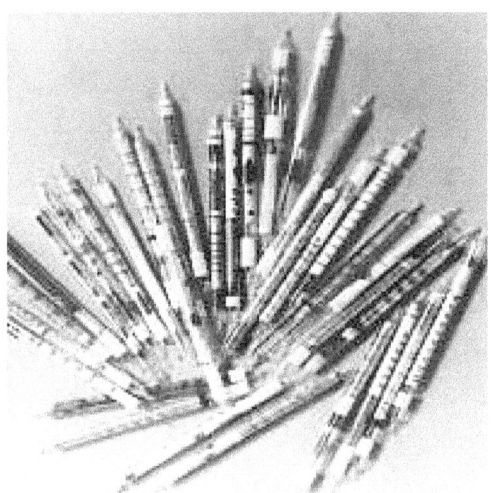

Figure 3-5. Draeger Tubes

3.1.6 Surface Acoustic Wave (SAW)

Surface acoustic wave detectors consist of piezoelectric crystals coated with a film designed to absorb chemical agents from the air. SAW detectors use 2 to 6 piezoelectric crystals that are coated with different polymeric films. Each polymeric film preferentially absorbs a particular class of volatile compound. For example, one polymeric film will be designed to preferentially absorb water, while other polymer films are designed to preferentially absorb different types of chemicals such as trichloroethylene, toluene, ethyl-benzene, or formaldehyde. The piezoelectric crystals detect the mass of the chemical vapors absorbed into the different, chemically selective polymeric coatings. The change in mass of the polymeric coatings causes the resonant frequency of the piezoelectric crystal to change. By monitoring the resonant frequency of the different piezoelectric crystals, a response pattern of the system for a particular vapor is generated. This response pattern is then stored in a microprocessor. When the system is operating, it constantly compares each new response pattern to the stored response pattern for the target vapor. When the response pattern for the target vapor matches the stored pattern, the system alarm is activated. The selectivity and sensitivity of these detectors depends on the ability of the film to absorb only the suspect chemical agents from the sample air. Many SAW devices use preconcentration tubes to reduce environmental interferences and increase the detection sensitivity. A detector manufactured by Microsensor Systems, Incorporated that is based upon the SAW technology is the SAW Minicad II (Figure 3-6).

Figure 3-6. SAW Minicad II

3.1.7 Photo Ionization Detection (PID)

Photo ionization detectors work by exposing a gas stream to an ultraviolet light of a wavelength with energy sufficient to ionize an agent molecule. If agents are present in the gas stream, they are ionized. An ion detector then registers a voltage proportional to the number of ions produced in the gas sample and thus the concentration of the agent. Specificity of these detectors is a function of how narrow the spectral range of the exciting radiation is and on how unique that energy is to ionizing only the molecule of interest. Rae Systems produces the MINIRAE Plus, a handheld detector that utilizes the PID technology. Another handheld PID detector is the Photovac 2020 manufactured by Perkin-Elmer. These detectors are shown in Figures 3-7 and 3-8.

Figure 3-7. MINIRAE Plus

Figure 3-8. Photovac 2020 PID Monitor

3.1.8 Sensor Array Technology

Sensor array technology (SAT) devices are based upon the use of an array of several different chemical sensors such as conductive polymer, metal oxide, bulk acoustic wave (BAW) and SAW devices used simultaneously for real time monitoring. The various sensors that are used must respond rapidly and reversibly to the chemical vapors they are exposed to. This technology is used in instruments commonly known as electronic noses. One mobile laboratory detector that is based upon SAT is the EEV eNose 5000 Electronic Nose (shown in Figure 3-9).

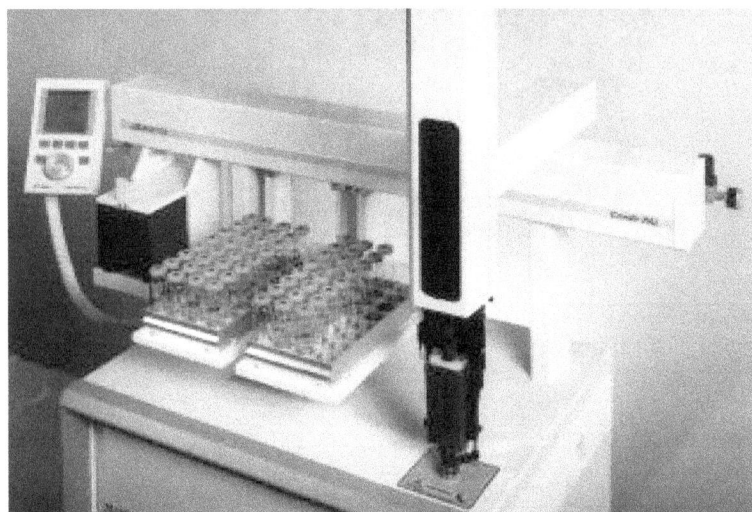

Figure 3-9. EEV eNose 5000 Electronic Nose

3.1.9 Thermal and Electrical Conductivity

Thermal and electrical conductivity detectors use metal oxide thermal conductivity semiconductors that measure the change in heat conductivity that occurs as a result of gas adsorption on the metal oxide surface. Also, the change in resistance and electrical conductivity across a metal foil in the system is measured when a gas adsorbs onto the surface of the metal film. Contaminants in the atmosphere being measured will result in measurable electrical differences from the "clean" or background atmosphere. Additionally, different contaminants will have different thermal conductivities and, therefore, different electrical responses from thermal and electrical conductivity detectors.

3.1.10 Flame Ionization

A flame ionization detector (FID) is a general-purpose detector used to determine the presence of volatile carbon-based compounds that are incinerated in a hydrogen-oxygen flame. When the carbonaceous compounds burn, an increase in the flame's baseline ion current takes place and detection of a compound occurs. FIDs are not specific and require separation technology for specificity, such as a gas chromatograph. Identification of compounds is generally determined by comparison of a compound's chromatographic retention time to that of a known standard, or to chromatographic retention indices for a series of known compounds using a standard set of chromatographic conditions. Perkin-Elmer manufactures a handheld FID, the MicroFID, for the nonspecific determination of flammable and potentially hazardous compounds in the concentration range of 0.1 to 50,000 ppm. The MicroFID is shown in Figure 3-10.

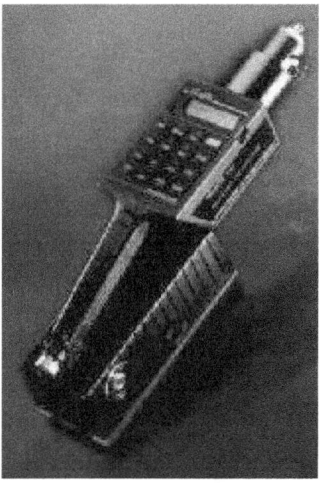

Figure 3-10. Perkin-Elmer
MicroFID Handheld Detector

3.2 Standoff Detectors (Infrared Spectroscopy)

Standoff detectors are used to give advance warning of a chemical agent cloud. Standoff detectors typically use optimal spectroscopy and can detect chemical agents at distances as great as 5 kilometers. Agent-free spectra must be used as a baseline to compare with freshly measured spectra that may contain chemical agent. Standoff detectors are generally difficult to operate and usually require the operator to have some knowledge of spectroscopy in order to interpret results. Available standoff detectors use infrared spectroscopy with either passive or active sensing.

3.2.1 Passive (Forward Looking Infrared (FLIR), Fourier Transform Infrared (FTIR))

Passive standoff detectors collect infrared radiation emitted and/or measure infrared radiation absorbed from the background to detect chemical agent and TIM vapor clouds. Passive standoff detectors employ one of two infrared spectroscopy technologies: (1) forward looking infrared (FLIR) imager or (2) Fourier Transform Infrared (FTIR) spectrometer in order to collect the infrared radiation. The difference between the two is how they process the infrared radiation. FLIR spectroscopy uses a series of optical filters, and FTIR spectroscopy uses an interferometer.

3.2.2 Active (Differential Absorption LIDAR)

Light detection and ranging (LIDAR) is the laser analog to radar. In LIDAR, a pulsed laser beam is sent out to a target object. Some of the light that is incident on the target is reflected back to the sender, and the rest is scattered, reflected, transmitted or absorbed by the medium. The time it takes for the light to travel from the sender to the target and back to the sender is used to calculate the distance to the target. For studying clouds in the atmosphere, differential absorption LIDAR can be used to measure both the range of the cloud and the concentration profile of the cloud. In differential absorption LIDAR, two laser beams of slightly different frequency are used to analyze the cloud.

One of the frequencies is tuned to a molecular absorption of one of the molecules in the cloud (this requires prior knowledge of cloud composition). The intensity of the reflected beam is a function of the amount of laser light absorbed by the cloud. This is related to the concentration of the absorbing molecule in the cloud. The cloud does not absorb the second frequency. Since its frequency is similar to that of the first laser, it will have a similar reflection and scatter profile. Thus the difference in the intensity of the two reflected beams will be due to absorption of the first laser beam by the cloud. The intensity of the return signal from the second laser beam is used as a baseline for calculating concentrations in the cloud. The time it takes for the two lasers to reflect back to the sender is used to calculate the range of the cloud. LIDAR is useful for tracking a chemical agent cloud once it has been identified but typically can not be used to identify a chemical agent cloud.

3.3   Analytical Instruments

The analytical instruments described in this section can be used to analyze samples as small as a few micro liters or milligrams. They are designed to differentiate between and accurately measure the unique chemical properties of different molecules. These instruments are quite sophisticated in order to detect and differentiate subtle differences between trace amounts of different molecules. Accuracy and reliability requires that only very pure reagents are used and that very rigid protocol and operating procedures are followed. This typically precludes their use outside of a laboratory environment that is staffed by technically trained people. However, some analytical instruments have been developed for field applications. Additionally, the instruments do not display the measured data in a straightforward manner. Interpretation of the measured data typically requires a technical background and extensive formal training.

3.3.1   Mass Spectrometry (MS)

Mass spectrometry is a technique that can positively identify a chemical agent at very low concentrations. In this technique, a volatilized sample is ionized, typically by an electron beam, which also causes the molecule to fragment into smaller ionized pieces. The ionized molecules and fragments are then passed into a mass analyzer that uses electric fields to separate the ions according to the ratio of their mass divided by their electric charge. The analyzer allows only ions of the same mass over charge ratio to impinge upon the detector. By scanning the electric potentials in the mass analyzer, all the different mass/charge ions can be detected. The result is a mass spectrum that shows the relative amount and the mass of each fragment, and the un-fragmented parent molecule. Since each molecule forms a unique set of fragments, mass spectroscopy provides positive identification. To simplify interpretation of the mass spectrum, it is best to introduce only one compound at a time. This is often achieved by using a gas chromatograph to separate the components in the sample. The end of the gas chromatography column is connected directly to the inlet of the mass spectrometer. Two instruments that use mass spectrometry are the Inficon Hapsite® Field Portable System and the Agilent 6890-5973 GC/MSD shown in Figures 3-11 and 3-12 respectively.

22

Figure 3-11. Inficon Hapsite® Field Portable System

Figure 3-12. Agilent 6890-5973 GC/MSD

3.3.2 Gas Chromatography (GC)

The gas chromatograph uses an inert gas to transport a sample of air through a long chromatographic column. Each molecule sticks to the column with a different amount of force and does not travel down the column at the same speed as the carrier gas. This causes the chemical agents and interferants to come out the end of the column at different times (called the retention time). Since the retention time is known for the chemical agents, the signal from an associated detector is only observed for a short period starting before and ending just after the retention time of the chemical agent. This eliminates false alarms from similar compounds that have different retention times. Using a pre-concentrator specific to the analyte can also reduce false alarms caused by interferants. The pre-concentrator passes air through an absorbent filter that traps agent molecules. The filter is then isolated from the air and heated to release any chemical agent that may have been trapped. The released chemical agent is then pumped through the column and the detector. Two instruments that use gas chromatography are the Perkin-Elmer Voyager and the Sentex Systems, Incorporated Scentograph Plus II shown in Figures 3-13 and 3-14 respectively.

Figure 3-13. Perkin-Elmer Voyager

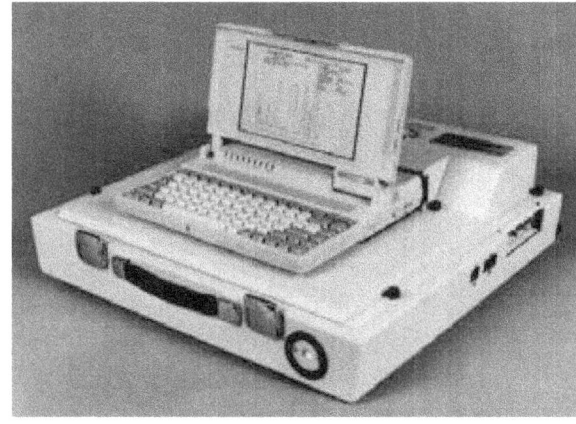

Figure 3-14. Sentex Systems, Incorporated Scentograph Plus II

3.3.3 High Performance Liquid Chromatography (HPLC)

High performance liquid chromatography is most useful in the detection and identification of larger molecular weight chemical agents such as BZ or LSD, and in the detection and identification of biological agents. With HPLC, those compounds that do not easily volatilize can be analyzed without undergoing chemical derivatization. HPLC instrumentation is available from a variety of vendors such as Hewlett Packard, Perkin-Elmer, Shimadzu, and Varian, and is shown in Figures 3-15, 3-16, 3-17, and 3-18. As with GCs, HPLC instruments can be equipped with a variety of detectors such as ultraviolet–visible (uV-Vis) spectrometers, mass spectrometers, fluorescence spectrometers, and electrochemical detectors. Two limitations to the fielding of HPLCs and their detectors are the need for power requirements (120V house current) and high purity solvents. Currently there is no portable HPLC unit available.

Figure 3-15. Hewlett Packard HP1000 HPLC System

Figure 3-16. Perkin-Elmer Turbo LC Plus HPLC System

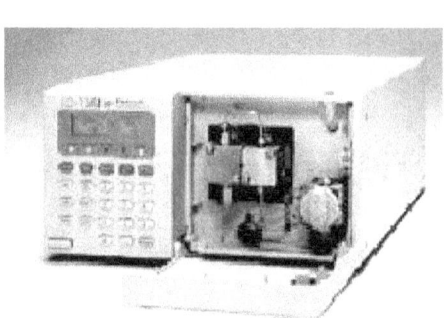

Figure 3-17. Shimadzu LC-10 HPLC System

Figure 3-18. Varian ProStar Analytical HPLC System

3.3.4 Ion Chromatography (IC)

Closely related to HPLC is a chromatographic technique known as ion chromatography (IC) where ionic species can be separated, detected and identified. IC instruments are available from Dionex and Brinkmann. Both instruments are shown in Figures 3-19 and 3-20 respectively. IC has been successfully used in the U.S. Army Materiel Command's Treaty Verification Laboratory in the analysis of several chemical nerve agents and their degradation products. As with HPLC, IC instruments require power requirements (120V house current), high purity water, and high purity chemical reagents for the preparation of buffering solutions.

Like HPLC, IC instruments can use uV-Vis spectrometers, mass spectrometers, and electrochemical detectors.

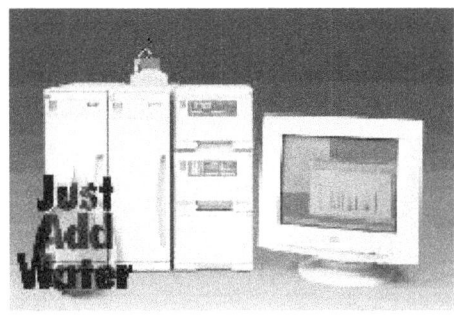

Figure 3-19. Dionex DX-500 IC System

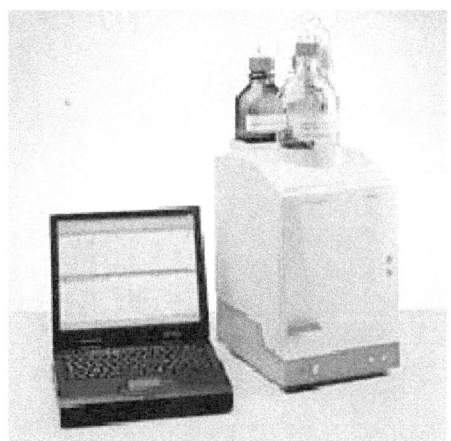

Figure 3-20. Brinkmann Metrohm Model 1761 IC System

3.3.5 Capillary Zone Electrophoresis

Capillary zone electrophoresis (CZE or CE) is a chromatographic technique that can be thought of as a hybridization of gas chromatography, liquid chromatography, and ion chromatography. Rather than using a temperature gradient or a solvent gradient (as in GC or HPLC, respectively), a mobile phase containing an ionic buffer is used (as in ion chromatography). A high voltage electric field (either fixed potential or a gradient) is applied across a fused silica column similar to capillary columns used in GC.

Hewlett Packard manufactures the model HP^{3D} CZE System, Beckman-Coulter manufactures the model P/ACE™ 5000 CZE System, and Bio-Rad manufactures the BioFocus 2000 CZE System. CZE instruments are typically configured with either a uV-Vis spectrometer or an electrochemical detector, but it can be interfaced to a mass spectrometer. Capillary zone electrophoresis instrumentation shares the same electrical requirements as HPLC and IC instruments. However, the need for high purity water and chemical reagents is still there but in much smaller quantities. These systems are shown in Figures 3-21, 3-22, and 3-23.

Figure 3-21. Hewlett-Packard HP^{3D} CZE System

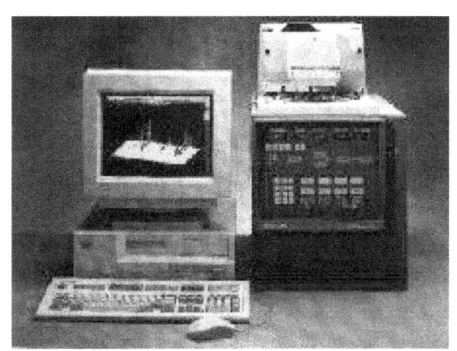

Figure 3-22. Beckman-Coulter P/ACE™ 5000 CZE System

25

Figure 3-23. Bio-Rad BioFocus 2000 CZE System

SECTION 4.0
SELECTION FACTORS

Section 4.0 provides a discussion of sixteen selection factors that are recommended for consideration by the emergency first responder community when selecting and purchasing chemical agent and TIM detection equipment. These factors were compiled by a panel of experienced scientists and engineers with multiple years of experience in chemical agent and TIM detection and analysis, domestic preparedness, and identification of emergency first responder needs. The factors have also been shared with the emergency first responder community in order to obtain their thoughts and comments.

It is anticipated that, as additional input is received from the emergency first responder community, additional factors may be added or existing factors may be modified. These factors were developed so that chemical agent and TIM detection equipment could be compared and contrasted in order to assist with the selection and purchase of the most appropriate equipment. *It is important to note that the evaluation conducted using the sixteen selection factors was based upon vendor-supplied data and no independent evaluation of equipment was conducted in the development of this guide.* The vendor-supplied data can be found in its entirety in Volume II. The results of the evaluation of the detection equipment against the sixteen selection factors are provided in section 5.0. The remainder of this section defines each of the selection factors. Details on the manner in which the selection factors were used to assess the detectors are presented in Table 4-1.

4.1   Chemical Agents Detected

This factor describes the ability of the equipment to detect chemical agents. Chemical agents, when referred to in this guide, refer to nerve and blister agents only. Blood agents and choking agents are included within the list of TIMs. Nerve agents primarily consist of GB and VX. Other nerve agents include GA, GD, and GF. Blister agents are primarily limited to mustard (H). Other blister agents considered in this guide include HD, HN, and L.

4.2   TIMs Detected

This factor describes the ability of the equipment to detect TIMs. TIMs considered in the development of this guide are discussed in section 2.2 and identified in one of three hazard indices (Table 2-4).

4.3   Sensitivity

Sensitivity is the lowest concentration a chemical agent or TIM can be detected at by a detector or instrument. This is also referred to as the detection limit. Detection limits may be dependent upon the chemical agent or TIM, the environmental conditions, or operational conditions.

Immediately dangerous to life and health (IDLH) is defined as the concentration at which self-contained breathing apparatus (SCBA) or respirators must be worn or immediate life threatening effects will occur. The purpose of establishing an IDLH exposure level is to ensure that the worker can escape from a given contaminated environment in the event of a failure of the respiratory protection equipment. IDLH values for the chemical agents and most of the 98 TIMs that are listed are provided in Volume II, Appendix D.

This guide bases its assessment of the sensitivity evaluation factors on the IDLH of chemical agents and TIMs versus the detection range of a detector. This factor does not apply to M8 and M9 paper since they require liquid contact to determine the presence of chemical agents or TIMs.

4.4   Resistance to Interferants

An interferant is a compound that causes a detector to either false alarm or fail to alarm. This factor describes the ability of a detector or instrument to resist the effects of interferants.

4.5   Response Time

Response time is defined as the time it takes for an instrument to collect a sample, analyze the sample, determine if an agent is present, and provide feedback.

4.6   Start-up Time

The start-up time is the time required for setting up and initiating sampling with an instrument.

4.7   Detection States

This factor indicates the sample states that an instrument can detect. The sample states include vapor, aerosol, and liquid.

4.8   Alarm Capability

This factor indicates if an instrument has an audible, visible, or audible/visible alarm.

4.9   Portability

Portability is the ability of the equipment to be transported including any support equipment required to operate the device. Two important things to consider under portability are the equipment dimensions and its weight. They determine if a single person can transport the equipment or if the equipment requires vehicular transport.

4.10 Power Capabilities

Power capabilities indicate whether specific equipment components can operate on a battery and/or AC electrical power.

4.11 Battery Needs

Battery power is the ability of the equipment to be powered by batteries with an operating life capable of sustaining activities throughout an incident. The number of batteries required for operation is also an important consideration.

4.12 Operational Environment

This factor describes the type of environment required by the equipment to operate optimally. For example, some equipment is designed to operate in the field under common outdoor weather conditions and climates, i.e., extreme temperatures, humidity, rain, snow, fog, etc. However, other equipment may require more climate controlled conditions such as a laboratory environment.

4.13 Durability

The durability of a piece of equipment describes how rugged the equipment is, i.e., how well can the equipment withstand rough handling and still operate.

4.14 Procurement Costs

Unit cost is the cost of the piece of equipment including the cost of all support equipment and consumables.

4.15 Operator Skill Level

Operator skill level refers to the skill level and training required for the operation of an instrument.

4.16 Training Requirements

Training requirements is the amount of time required to instruct the operator to become proficient in the operation of the instrument. For example, higher end equipment such as ion mobility spectrometers or SAW device requires more in-depth training such as specialized classes for operation, maintenance, and calibration of the equipment.

Table 4-1. Selection Factor Key For Chemical Detection Equipment
May 2000

Selection Factor	●	◕	◑	◔	○
Chemical Agents Detected	Detects all nerve and blister agents		Detects either the nerve or blister agent class		Detects none of the nerve or blister agents
TIMs Detected	Detects all of the TIMs listed	Detects multiple TIMs	Detects one TIM		Detects none of the TIMs listed
Sensitivity	Detects at one-tenth IDLH for all detectable chemicals	Detects at one-tenth IDLH for one or more detectable chemicals	Detects at IDLH for all detectable chemicals	Detects at IDLH for one or more detectable chemicals	Does not detect IDLH levels
Resistance to Interferents	Responds only to chemical agents and TIMs	Has a few non-critical interferents		Has many interferents	Does not discriminate between chemical agents/TIMs and interferents
Response Time	Less than 10 seconds	Between 10 and 60 seconds		Between 60 seconds and 2 minutes	Greater than 2 minutes
Start-Up Time	Less than 30 seconds	Between 30 and 60 seconds	Between 1 and 5 minutes	Between 5 and 30 minutes	More than 30 minutes
Detection States	Detects chemicals in all three states	Detects chemicals in two states	Detects chemicals in one state		No capability
Alarm Capability	Audible and Visible alarm	Audible alarm only	Visible alarm only	No capability	No capability
Portability	Less than 2 pounds and handheld	Between 2 and 5 pounds and handheld	Between 5 and 10 pounds	Between 10 and 50 pounds	Greater than 50 pounds
Battery Needs	Operates on standard, inexpensive, and readily available batteries for eight hours of continuous use		Operates on standard, inexpensive, and readily available batteries for two hours of continuous use		Operates on special order and expensive batteries
Power Capabilities	Battery or AC Powered	Battery Powered		Vehicle or AC Powered	AC Powered
Environment	Operates in all expected environments		Operates in most environments		Operation is restricted to certain environments
Durability	Able to operate with rough handling		Able to operate after being moved but not after rough handling		Must remain stationary
Unit Cost	Less than $500 per unit	Between $500 and $2000 per unit	Between $2000 and $5000 per unit		More than $5000 per unit
Operator Skills	No special skills or training required		No special skills but training required		Technician required to operate equipment
Training	No special training required		Less than 8 hours training required		More than 8 hours training required

The gray cells designate that the symbol is not applicable for the selection factor.
A duplicate of this table is provided for quick reference (as Table 5-13).

30

SECTION 5.0
EQUIPMENT EVALUATION

The market survey (refer to section 2.0 of volume II) conducted for chemical agent and TIM detection equipment identified 148 different pieces of detection equipment. The details of the market survey to include data on each piece of equipment are provided in Volume II of this guide. Section 5.0 documents the results of evaluating each equipment item versus the sixteen selection factors. Section 5.1 defines the equipment usage categories and section 5.2 discusses the evaluation results.

5.1   Equipment Usage Categories

In order to display the evaluation results in a meaningful format, the detection equipment was grouped into six categories based on the prospective manner of usage by the emergency first responder community. These usage categories included the following:

- handheld-portable
- handheld-stationary
- vehicle mounted
- fixed-site analytical
- fixed-site detection system
- standoff

The definitions for the six usage categories were extracted from the *Final Report on Chemical Detection Equipment Market Survey for Emergency Responders*. (See detailed reference in Appendix B). The definitions for each of the usage categories are as follows:

- **Handheld-Portable.** Equipment defined as being human portable for mobile operations in the field. The instrument is light enough to be carried by an emergency first responder and operated while moving through a building.

- **Handheld-Stationary.** Equipment defined as being human portable for stationary operations. The instrument is light enough to be carried by an emergency first responder but can only be operated while stationary.

- **Vehicle-Mounted.** Equipment defined as being used in or from a mobile vehicle and generally uses vehicle battery for power requirements. The equipment is designed for monitoring inside or within the general vicinity of a vehicle.

- **Fixed-Site Detection Systems.** Equipment defined as stand-alone detection systems specifically designed to operate inside a building. The duration of operation for these instruments is indefinite, and the power requirements are met through the building infrastructure. Consumables required for continuous operation of the detection instruments would need to be provided by the building management (i.e., compressed gas cylinders).

- **Fixed-Site Analytical Systems.** Equipment defined as stand-alone detection systems requiring a means of delivering a sample to the equipment for analysis. This equipment generally requires a trained technical operator as well as extensive labor to assemble and disassemble inside a building for short duration monitoring of an area. This equipment typically performs low level monitoring of an area but has not been specifically designed for use outside a laboratory.

- **Standoff Detector Systems.** Equipment specifically designed to monitor the presence of chemical agents and TIMs that may be present in the atmosphere up to three miles away. These systems typically require one or two individuals for monitoring operations. Depending on the technique employed and the environmental conditions, these detectors can have high or low selectivity. Standoff detectors usually require vehicle transport and special setup.

The results of categorizing the chemical agent (CA) and TIM detection equipment are detailed in Table 5-1. Equipment was also categorized by its detection capability (chemical agents, TIMs, or both).

Table 5-1. Detection Equipment Usage Categories

Detector Type	Detection Capability			
	Chemical Agents	TIMs	Both	Total
Handheld-Portable	12	52	5	69
Handheld-Stationary	15	12	12	39
Vehicle-Mounted	5	0	0	5
Fixed-Site Detection Systems	8	0	0	8
Fixed-Site Analytical	23	0	0	23
Standoff Detectors	4	0	0	4
Total	**67**	**64**	**17**	**148**

5.2   Evaluation Results

The evaluation results for the chemical agent and TIM detection equipment are presented in tabular format for the 148 pieces of detection equipment identified at the time of the writing of this guide. A table is presented for each of the six usage categories with the handheld-portable and handheld-stationary detectors subdivided by detection capability. Each table includes the specific equipment and the symbol that corresponds to how the equipment item was characterized based upon each of the selection factor definitions. If data was not available to characterize a specific selection factor, the acronym 'TBD' is displayed in the appropriate cell. If a selection factor is not appropriate for a specific equipment item, the acronym 'NA' is used to characterize that selection factor. Table 5-2 provides the table number and associated table pages for each of the usage categories.

Table 5-2. Evaluation Results Reference Table

Table Name	Table Number	Page(s)
Handheld-Portable (CAs)	5-3	35-36
Handheld-Portable (TIMs)	5-4	37-43
Handheld-Portable (Both)	5-5	44
Handheld -Stationary (CAs)	5-6	45-46
Handheld -Stationary (TIMs)	5-7	47-48
Handheld -Stationary (Both)	5-8	49-50
Vehicle-Mounted	5-9	51
Fixed-Site Detection Systems	5-10	52
Fixed-Site Analytical	5-11	53-55
Standoff Detectors	5-12	56
Selection Factor Key	5-13	57

5.2.1   Handheld-Portable Detection Equipment.

There were 69 handheld-portable detectors identified in the development of this guide. These 69 detectors were further divided into three subcategories identifying their detection capability. There were 12 handheld-portable detectors capable of detecting chemical agents only. There were 52 handheld-portable detectors capable of detecting one or more of the 98 TIMs. There were 5 handheld-portable detectors capable of detecting both chemical agents and TIMs. Tables 5-3, 5-4, and 5-5 detail the evaluation results for all three of these subcategories respectively.

5.2.2   Handheld-Stationary Detection Equipment.

There were 39 handheld-stationary detectors identified in the development of this guide. These 39 detectors were further divided into three subcategories identifying their detection capability. There were 15 handheld-stationary detectors capable of detecting chemical agents only. There were 12 detectors capable of detecting one or more of the 98 TIMs. There were 12 detectors capable of detecting both chemical agents and TIMs. Tables 5-6, 5-7, and 5-8 detail the evaluation results for all three of these subcategories.

5.2.3   Vehicle-Mounted Detection Equipment.

There were 5 vehicle-mounted detection equipment items identified in the development of this guide. Table 5-9 details the results of the vehicle-mounted equipment evaluation.

5.2.4   Fixed-Site Detection Systems.

There were 8 fixed-site detection systems identified in the development of this guide. Table 5-10 details the results of the fixed-site detection system evaluation.

5.2.5 Fixed-Site Analytical Laboratory Systems.

There were 23 fixed-site analytical equipment items identified in the development of this guide. Nine of the 23 pieces of equipment identified in this category have very little vendor data available. Most of the data fields are labeled with 'TBD'. It is anticipated that this data will be available in the next revision to this guide. Table 5-11 details the results of the fixed-site analytical equipment evaluation.

5.2.6 Standoff Detection Systems.

There were 4 standoff detectors identified in the development of this guide. Table 5-12 details the results of the standoff detector evaluation.

Table 5-3. Handheld Portable Detection Equipment (CA)
May 2000

ID #	Detector Name	Chemical Agents Detected	TIMs Detected	Sensitivity	Resistance to Interferents	Response Time	Start-Up Time	Detection States	Alarm Capability	Portability	Battery Needs	Power Capabilities	Environment	Durability	Unit Cost	Operator Skills	Training
3	Chemical Agent Monitor (CAM), Ion Mobility Spectrometry												TBD				
5	Improved Chemical Agent Monitor-Advanced Portable Detector (ICAM-APD)												TBD	TBD			
8	M90-D1 Chemical Warfare Agent Detector IMS											TBD	TBD				
11	APACC Chemical Control Alarm Portable Apparatus (Model M266 E 10 002)											TBD	TBD				
16	Automatic Liquid Agent Detector (ALAD) System			TBD		TBD						TBD	TBD	TBD			
27	SAW Minicad II Surface Acoustic Wave												TBD				
28	Photovac Microtip Handheld Air Monitor/Photoionization Detector		TBD						TBD			TBD	TBD	TBD			

'NA' - the specific selection factor is not applicable for the piece of equipment.
'TBD' (to be determined) - there is currently no data available to support that selection factor.
See Table 5-13 for selection factor definitions.

Table 5-3. Handheld Portable Detection Equipment (CA)
May 2000

ID #	Detector Name	Chemical Agents Detected	TIMs Detected	Sensitivity	Resistance to Interferents	Response Time	Start-Up Time	Detection States	Alarm Capability	Portability	Battery Needs	Power Capabilities	Environment	Durability	Unit Cost	Operator Skills	Training
30	MiniRae 2000	●	TBD	○	TBD	◐	◐	●	●	●	◕	◐	TBD	◐	◐	◐	●
60	AP2C Chemical Agent Detector	●	○	◔	◕	◐	●	●	●	◐	●	◕	●	●	○	●	●	●
77	MSA Passport II PID Monitor	TBD	◐	○	TBD	TBD	TBD	◐	TBD	TBD	TBD	TBD	TBD	TBD	○	◐	TBD
84	Advanced Portable Detector (APD) 2000	●	●	◔	◔	◕	◕	◐	●	◐	●	●	●	TBD	○	◐	◐
154	DET INDIV Individual Nerve Agent Detector	◐	◐	◕	◕	◐	◔	◐	○	TBD	NA	NA	●	●	TBD	●	●	●

'NA' - the specific selection factor is not applicable for the piece of equipment.
'TBD' (to be determined) - there is currently no data available to support that selection factor.
See Table 5-13 for selection factor definitions.

Table 5-4. Handheld Portable Detection Equipment (TIMs)
May 2000

ID #	Detector Name	Chemical Agents Detected	TIMs Detected	Sensitivity	Resistance to Interferents	Response Time	Start-Up Time	Detection States	Alarm Capability	Portability	Battery Needs	Power Capabilities	Environment	Durability	Unit Cost	Operator Skills	Training
39	(SCX) SXC-20 VOC Monitor Thermal and Electrical Conductivity	○	◐	●	◔	●	◐	●	◔	●	●	TBD	TBD	◔	◐	◐	●
63	Kitagawa Gas Detector Tubes	○	◔	◔	◔	●	◐	○	●	NA	NA	●	●	●	●	●	●
64	Sensidyne Gas Detection Tubes	○	◔	TBD	TBD	●	◐	○	TBD	NA	NA	●	●	●	●	●	●
78	MicroFID Handheld Detector	○	TBD	○	●	◐	◐	●	◐	●	◔	◐	●	●	○	●	●
81	Chrom Air Badges	○	◔	TBD	◔	●	◐	◐	●	NA	NA	TBD	●	TBD	TBD	●	●
82	SureSpot Badges	○	◔	◔	◔	●	◐	◐	●	NA	NA	◐	TBD	TBD	●	●	●
95	ToxiRae Plus Personal Gas Monitor	○	◔	◔	○	TBD	◐	●	●	●	●	◐	●	●	◔	●	◐
100	Neotox-XL Single Gas Monitor	○	◔	◔	TBD	TBD	◐	●	●	●	◔	●	●	TBD	●	●	◐

'NA' - the specific selection factor is not applicable for the piece of equipment.
'TBD' (to be determined) - there is currently no data available to support that selection factor.
See Table 5-13 for selection factor definitions.

Table 5-4. Handheld Portable Detection Equipment (TIMs)
May 2000

ID #	Detector Name	Chemical Agents Detected	TIMs Detected	Sensitivity	Resistance to Interferents	Response Time	Start-Up Time	Detection States	Alarm Capability	Portability	Battery Needs	Power Capabilities	Environment	Durability	Unit Cost	Operator Skills Training
103	Omni-4000 Gas Detector	○	◕	◔	◔	TBD	◑	●	◔	●	◔	◑	●	TBD	●	◑
104	AutoStep Plus	○	◕	◕	◕	◑	◑	◕	◑	●	◔	◑	●	◑	●	●
108	Spectrum Electrochemistry	○	◕	◔	◔	TBD	●	◔	●	●	◔	◑	●	TBD	●	◑
109	Logic 400 series (Model 450) Personal Air Monitor	○	◕	◕	TBD	TBD	◑	●	●	●	◕	◑	TBD	TBD	●	◑
112	TLV Panther Gas Detector	○	◑	TBD	◔	◕	◑	●	◑	●	◔	◑	●	◑	◑	◑
113	FoxTox Personal Multi-Gas Monitor	○	◕	◔	○	TBD	◑	◕	●	●	◔	◑	●	TBD	●	◑
114	Pac III Single Gas Detector	○	◕	◔	TBD	TBD	◑	●	●	●	◔	◑	●	◔	●	◑
115	LTX312 Gas Monitor	○	◑	◔	◕	●	◑	◕	●	●	◔	◑	●	◔	●	◑

'NA' - the specific selection factor is not applicable for the piece of equipment.
'TBD' (to be determined) - there is currently no data available to support that selection factor.
See Table 5-13 for selection factor definitions.

Table 5-4. Handheld Portable Detection Equipment (TIMs)
May 2000

ID #	Detector Name	Chemical Agents Detected	TIMs Detected	Sensitivity	Resistance to Interferents	Response Time	Start-Up Time	Detection States	Alarm Capability	Portability	Battery Needs	Power Capabilities	Environment	Durability	Unit Cost	Operator Skills Training
116	PortaSens II Gas Detector					TBD										
117	MultiRae Plus Gas Detector					TBD										
118	Bodyguard 4 Personal Monitor													TBD		
119	PhD2 Personal Gas Detector		TWA		TBD	TBD						TBD				
120	Haz-Alert Gas Detector		TBD		TBD							TBD				
121	Tox-Array 1000 Gas Detector		TBD			TBD								TBD		
122	AMC Series 1100 Portable Gas Detector															
123	MultiLog 2000 Multi-Gas Monitor															

'NA' - the specific selection factor is not applicable for the piece of equipment.
'TBD' (to be determined) - there is currently no data available to support that selection factor.
See Table 5-13 for selection factor definitions.

39

Table 5-4. Handheld Portable Detection Equipment (TIMs)

May 2000

ID #	Detector Name	Chemical Agents Detected	TIMs Detected	Sensitivity	Resistance to Interferents	Response Time	Start-Up Time	Detection States	Alarm Capability	Portability	Battery Needs	Power Capabilities	Environment	Durability	Unit Cost	Operator Skills	Training
124	IQ-250 Single Gas Detector	○	◕	TBD	◔	◔	TBD	◐	●	●	●	◐	●	◕	●	◐	
126	MiniGas-XL Multi-gas Monitor	○	◕	◐	◔	TBD	TBD	◐	●	●	●	◐	●	TBD	●	◐	
127	Toxibee Personal Gas Alarm	○	◕	◐	◔	●	TBD	◐	●	TBD	TBD	◐	TBD	TBD	●	◐	
128	MicroPac Personal Gas Alarm	○	◕	◐	◔	◔	◔	◐	●	●	◕	◐	●	●	●	◐	
129	Toxi Gas Detector	○	◕	TBD	◔	TBD	TBD	◐	●	●	◕	TBD	●	TBD	●	◐	
130	Toxi Plus Gas Detector	○	◕	TBD	◔	TBD	TBD	◐	●	●	◕	TBD	●	TBD	●	◐	
131	Toxi Ultra Gas Detector	○	◕	TBD	◔	TBD	TBD	◐	●	●	◕	TBD	●	TBD	●	◐	
132	TMX412 Multi-Gas Monitor	○	◕	◐	◔	◕	◕	◐	●	●	◕	◐	●	◐	●	◐	

'NA' - the specific selection factor is not applicable for the piece of equipment.
'TBD' (to be determined) - there is currently no data available to support that selection factor.
See Table 5-13 for selection factor definitions.

40

Table 5-4. Handheld Portable Detection Equipment (TIMs)
May 2000

ID #	Detector Name	Chemical Agents Detected	TIMs Detected	Sensitivity	Resistance to Interferents	Response Time	Start-Up Time	Detection States	Alarm Capability	Portability	Battery Needs	Power Capabilities	Environment	Durability	Unit Cost	Operator Skills	Training
133	ATX 612 Multi-Gas Aspirated Monitor																
134	T80 Single Gas Monitor																
135	Gas Badge Personal Gas Alarm																
136	Unimax Personal Single Gas Detector				TBD	TBD								TBD			
137	MicroMax Multigas Monitor				TBD	TBD								TBD			
138	MiniWarn Gas Detector				TBD	TBD								TBD			
139	Multiwarn II Gas Detector				TBD	TBD								TBD			
140	Smart Logger Gas Detector				TBD	TBD								TBD			

'NA' - the specific selection factor is not applicable for the piece of equipment.
'TBD' (to be determined) - there is currently no data available to support that selection factor.
See Table 5-13 for selection factor definitions.

Table 5-4. Handheld Portable Detection Equipment (TIMs)

May 2000

Symbol key used below: ○ = open, ◔ = quarter, ◑ = half, ◕ = three-quarter, ● = full; TBD = to be determined.

ID #	Detector Name	Chemical Agents Detected	TIMs Detected	Sensitivity	Resistance to Interferents	Response Time	Start-Up Time	Detection States	Alarm Capability	Portability	Battery Needs	Power Capabilities	Environment	Durability	Unit Cost	Operator Skills / Training
142	Target Gas Detector	○	◕	◔	◔	TBD	◑	●	●	●	◕	◑	●	TBD	●	◑
143	Quadrant Portable Gas Detector	○	◕	◔	◔	TBD	◑	●	●	●	◕	TBD	●	◑	●	◑
144	VRAE Hand Held 5 Gas Surveyor (Model 7800 Monitor)	○	◕	◔	TBD	TBD	◑	●	●	●	◕	◑	●	TBD	●	◑
147	GT Series Portable Gas Monitor	○	◕	◔	○	TBD	◑	●	◕	●	◕	◑	●	◑	●	◑
148	Genesis Portable Gas Monitor	○	◕	◔	◔	TBD	◑	●	●	●	◕	◑	●	◕	●	◑
149	95 Series Single Gas Monitor	○	◕	◔	◔	TBD	◑	●	●	●	◕	◑	●	●	●	◑
150	MultiCheck 2000 Multi-Gas Monitor	○	◕	◔	◔	◕	◑	●	●	●	◕	◑	●	◕	●	●
153	TX-2000 Toxic Gas Detector	○	◕	◔	TBD	TBD	◑	●	●	●	◕	◑	●	TBD	●	◑

'NA' - the specific selection factor is not applicable for the piece of equipment.
'TBD' (to be determined) - there is currently no data available to support that selection factor.
See Table 5-13 for selection factor definitions.

Table 5-4. Handheld Portable Detection Equipment (TIMs)
May 2000

ID #	Detector Name	Chemical Agents Detected	TIMs Detected	Sensitivity	Resistance to Interferents	Response Time	Start-Up Time	Detection States	Alarm Capability	Portability	Battery Needs	Power Capabilities	Environment	Durability	Unit Cost	Operator Skills Training
157	ProtectAir Personal Multi-Gas Monitor Model 8570	○	◔	TBD	TBD	●	◐	●	●	●	◔	◐	●	◔	●	◐
160	GasAlertMax	○	◐	TBD	◔	●	◐	●	●	●	◔	◔	●	◔	●	●
161	BW Defender	○	◐	TBD	◔	●	◐	●	●	●	◔	◔	●	◔	●	●
162	GasAlert	○	◔	TBD	◔	●	◐	●	●	●	◔	◔	●	◔	●	●

'NA' - the specific selection factor is not applicable for the piece of equipment.

'TBD' (to be determined) - there is currently no data available to support that selection factor.

See Table 5-13 for selection factor definitions.

43

Table 5-5. Handheld Portable Detection Equipment (CA and TIMs)
May 2000

ID #	Detector Name	Chemical Agents Detected	TIMs Detected	Sensitivity	Resistance to Interferents	Response Time	Start-Up Time	Detection States	Alarm Capability	Portability	Battery Needs	Power Capabilities	Environment	Durability	Unit Cost	Operator Skills	Training
4	Rapid Alarm & Identification Device-1 (RAID-1)	●	◐	◔	◔	◔	●	●	◐	●	●	●	TBD	○	●	●	◐
13	Individual (Improved) B35 Chemical Agent Detector (ICAD)	●	◔	◔	◔	●	◔	●	●	●	◔	◐	●	◐	●	●	◐
65	MSA Gas Detection Tubes	●	◔	◔	●	●	◔	◔	●	●	◔	●	◐	TBD	●	●	●
80	Photovac 2020 PID Monitor	TBD	TBD	○	○	◐	◔	◐	●	●	◔	◐	●	◐	◐	◐	●
159	Lightweight Chemical Detector (LCD-2)	●	◔	◔	◔	●	●	◔	●	●	◔	◐	●	●	○	●	◐

'NA' - the specific selection factor is not applicable for the piece of equipment.
'TBD' (to be determined) - there is currently no data available to support that selection factor.
See Table 5-13 for selection factor definitions.

Table 5-6. Handheld Stationary Detection Equipment (CA)
May 2000

Legend for data cells: ○ = empty, ◔ = quarter, ◑ = half, ◕ = three‑quarter, ● = full (Harvey balls); text values TBD and NA as noted.

ID #	Detector Name	Chemical Agents Detected	TIMs Detected	Sensitivity	Resistance to Interferents	Response Time	Start-Up Time	Detection States	Alarm Capability	Portability	Battery Needs	Power Capabilities	Environment	Durability	Unit Cost	Operator Skills	Training
2	M8A1 Automatic Chemical Agent Alarm	◑	○	◔	◔	◔	◑	●	◔	●	●	◑	●	TBD	◑	◑	◑
9	Phemtochem Ion Mobility Spectrometer, Model 110	●	TBD	◔	◔	○	◔	◕	◔	TBD	●	◑	TBD	●	●	◑	◑
17	ABC-M8 VGH Chemical Agent Detector Paper	●	○	◔	◕	●	◔	◑	●	NA	NA	◑	●	●	●	●	●
18	M9 Chemical Agent Detector Paper	●	○	◔	◕	●	◔	◑	●	NA	NA	◑	●	●	●	●	●
19	3-Way Paper, Chemical Agent Liquid Detectors	●	○	TBD	●	●	◑	◑	●	NA	NA	●	●	●	●	●	●
24	Nerve Agent Vapor Detector (NAVD)	●	◔	◔	●	●	◑	◑	●	NA	NA	TBD	TBD	●	●	●	●
25	No. 1 Mark 1 Detector Kit	●	◕	◕	TBD	◑	◕	◑	●	NA	NA	TBD	TBD	●	●	◑	◑
32	Scentograph Plus II Gas Chromatography	●	◔	TBD	◔	○	●	TBD	◔	TBD	◕	TBD	TBD	○	○	○	○

'NA' - the specific selection factor is not applicable for the piece of equipment.
'TBD' (to be determined) - there is currently no data available to support that selection factor.
See Table 5-13 for selection factor definitions.

45

Table 5-6. Handheld Stationary Detection Equipment (CA)
May 2000

ID #	Detector Name	Chemical Agents Detected	TIMs Detected	Sensitivity	Resistance to Interferents	Response Time	Start-Up Time	Detection States	Alarm Capability	Portability	Battery Needs	Power Capabilities	Environment	Durability	Unit Cost	Operator Skills	Training
50	Photovac Snapshot Hand Held Gas Chromatograph	●	○	TBD	○	◔	◕	◑	◔	TBD	◕	TBD	TBD	◕	○	○	
51	Scentoscreen (Gas Chromatography) with Argon Ionization Detector/ GC WITH MS	●	TBD	◔	○	◔	●	TBD	○	TBD	◕	TBD	TBD	○	○	○	
57	Gas Chromatograph with 4100 Vapor Detector	◑	○	●	◑	◔	◑	●	◔	NA	○	◑	TBD	◑	●	○	
58	Gas Chromatograph with 7100 Vapor Detector	◑	○	●	◕	◔	◑	●	◔	NA	○	◑	TBD	◑	●	○	
59	Century TVA-1000 Toxic Vapor Analyzer, Photoionization	●	TBD	TBD	●	TBD	◔	TBD	◔	●	◕	TBD	TBD	TBD	●	◑	
75	Hapsite Gas Chromatography with Mass Spectrometry	●	TBD	●	○	○	●	◕	◔	◑	●	◑	●	○	○	○	
83	Innova Type 1312 Multigas Monitor Photoacoustic Infrared Spectroscopy	●	TBD	●	◕	◔	◕	◕	◔	●	●	◑	TBD	○	◑	◑	

'NA' - the specific selection factor is not applicable for the piece of equipment.
'TBD' (to be determined) - there is currently no data available to support that selection factor.

46

Table 5-7. Handheld Stationary Detection Equipment (TIMs)
May 2000

ID #	Detector Name	Chemical Agents Detected	TIMs Detected	Sensitivity	Resistance to Interferents	Response Time	Start-up Time	Detection States	Alarm Capability	Portability	Battery Needs	Power Capabilities	Environment	Durability	Unit Cost	Operator Skills	Training
34	Portable Odor Monitor	○	◕	○	◔	●	◐	○	●	●	◕	◐	●	TBD	●	◐	
62	5-Step Field Identification Kit 8 Model 2000	○	TBD	TBD	TBD	TBD	◐	TBD	●	●	NA	TBD	TBD	◔	●	◐	
74	Voyager Gas Chromatography	○	◕	◔	○	◔	◐	●	◔	TBD	TBD	◐	●	○	○	○	
76	Electronic Reader Color Change Chemistry	○	◕	◔	TBD	◔	◐	●	TBD	TBD	NA	○	TBD	◔	●	◐	
99	Chemkey TLD Toxic Gas Monitor	○	◔	◔	TBD	TBD	◔	◐	●	◐	●	●	◐	TBD	TBD	●	◐	
101	Gas Beacon/Gas Leader	○	◔	◔	◔	TBD	TBD	◐	●	◔	●	◕	◐	●	TBD	●	◐	
102	Model 7100 Gas Monitor (Color Change Monitor)	○	◔	◐	TBD	◐	TBD	◐	●	○	NA	○	◐	◐	TBD	◐	◐	

'NA' - the specific selection factor is not applicable for the piece of equipment.
'TBD' (to be determined) - there is currently no data available to support that selection factor.
See Table 5-13 for selection factor definitions.

Table 5-7. Handheld Stationary Detection Equipment (TIMs)
May 2000

ID #	Detector Name	Chemical Agents Detected	TIMs Detected	Sensitivity	Resistance to Interferents	Response Time	Start-up Time	Detection States	Alarm Capability	Portability	Battery Needs	Power Capabilities	Environment	Durability	Unit Cost	Operator Skills	Training
110	SAFEYE Model 400 Gas Detection System	○	◕	◔	◕	●	◐	◐	◐	●	◕	◐	●	○	●	◐	
111	7000 Series Data Logging Compact Portable Gas Detector	○	◕	◔	◔	●	◐	●	◕	●	◕	◐	●	◐	●	◐	
125	CM4 Gas Monitor (Color Change Chemistry)	○	◕	TBD	◔	TBD	◐	●	○	NA	○	◐	TBD	TBD	◐	◐	
145	Gasman Portable Multiple Toxic Gas Monitor	○	◕	TBD	TBD	TBD	◐	TBD	TBD	TBD	TBD	TBD	TBD	TBD	◐	◐	
146	Model 680EZ Portable Photoionization Detector	○	TBD	TBD	TBD	TBD	◐	TBD	TBD	TBD	TBD	TBD	TBD	TBD	TBD	TBD	

'NA' - the specific selection factor is not applicable for the piece of equipment.
'TBD' (to be determined) - there is currently no data available to support that selection factor.
See Table 5-13 for selection factor definitions.

48

Table 5-8. Handheld Stationary Detection Equipment (CA and TIMs)
May 2000

ID #	Detector Name	Chemical Agents Detected	TIMs Detected	Sensitivity	Resistance to Interferents	Response Time	Start-Up Time	Detection States	Alarm Capability	Portability	Battery Needs	Power Capabilities	Environment	Durability	Unit Cost	Operator Skills
1	IMS 2000	●	◐	◕	◔	◐	◐	●	◔	●	●	TBD	TBD	○	◐	◐
6	Chemical Agent Monitor-2 (CAM-2) Ion Mobility Spectrometry	●	◕	◕	◕	●	●	◕	●	◔	●	●	●	●	○	●	◐
20	Chemical Agent Detector Kit	●	◕	◕	TBD	○	◐	TBD	NA	●	NA	NA	●	●	◕	●	◐
21	M18A2 Chemical Agent Detector Kit	●	◕	◔	◔	○	●	●	◐	◕	NA	NA	●	●	●	◐	◐
22	M256A1 Kit Color Change Chemistry	●	◔	◔	◔	○	●	◔	◐	●	NA	NA	●	●	●	●	●
23	M272 Water Kit Color Change	●	◐	◔	◕	○	●	◐	◐	◕	NA	NA	●	●	●	●	●
26	Draeger CDS Kit	●	◕	◔	TBD	○	◐	◔	○	●	NA	NA	◐	◐	◐	●	●

'NA' - the specific selection factor is not applicable for the piece of equipment.
'TBD' (to be determined) - there is currently no data available to support that selection factor.
See Table 5-13 for selection factor definitions.

49

Table 5-8. Handheld Stationary Detection Equipment (CA and TIMs)
May 2000

ID #	Detector Name	Chemical Agents Detected	TIMs Detected	Sensitivity	Resistance to Interferents	Response Time	Start-Up Time	Detection States	Alarm Capability	Portability	Battery Needs	Power Capabilities	Environment	Durability	Unit Cost	Operator Skills	Training
29	IS-101 Photoionization	●	◕	◔	TBD	●	●	◑	●	◔	TBD	◔	TBD	●	◑	◑	◑
35	Miran SaphIRe Portable Ambient Air Analyzer	●	◕	◑	TBD	◑	◑	◑	◔	◔	TBD	◔	TBD	●	●	○	◑
155	KDTC Color Change Chemistry	●	◕	◕	◔	◔	◔	◑	NA	●	TBD	◔	TBD	●	◑	○	○
156	RAPID I (Remote Air Pollution Infrared Detector)*	●	◕	◔	◑	◕	◑	◑	TBD	◔	●	●	TBD	●	●	◑	◑
160	ppbRae	●	◕	○	TBD	●	◑	◑	●	●	●	◔	◑	TBD	◑	◑	●

'NA' - the specific selection factor is not applicable for the piece of equipment.
'TBD' (to be determined) - there is currently no data available to support that selection factor.
See Table 5-13 for selection factor definitions.

50

Table 5-9. Vehicle-Mounted Detection Equipment
April 2000

ID #	Detector Name	Training	Operator Skills	Unit Cost	Durability	Environment	Power Capabilities	Battery Needs	Portability	Alarm Capability	Detection States	Start-Up Time	Response Time	Resistance to Interferents	Sensitivity	TIMs Detected	Chemical Agents Detected
36	Chemical Biological Mass Spectrometer (CBMS)	◐	●	○	●	●	◔	●	○	●	●	◔	●	●	◔	○	●
68	HP 6890 Series II GC with MS	○	○	TBD	○	TBD	○	NA	○	TBD	◐	TBD	○	TBD	TBD	TBD	●
69	MM-1 Mobile Mass Spectrometer Military	○	○	TBD	TBD	TBD	◔	●	○	TBD	●	○	○	◔	◔	○	●
70	EM-640 Mobile Mass Spectrometer Military	○	○	○	●	◐	●	●	○	TBD	●	◔	○	●	TBD	◔	●
79	eNOSE 5000 Electronic Nose Thermal and Electrical Conductivity	TBD	TBD	TBD	TBD	TBD	TBD	TBD	TBD	●	◐	TBD	TBD	TBD	TBD	TBD	TBD

'NA' - the specific selection factor is not applicable for the piece of equipment.
'TBD' (to be determined) - there is currently no data available to support that selection factor.
See Table 5-13 for selection factor definitions.

Table 5-10. Fixed-Site Detection Systems
May 2000

ID #	Detector Name	Chemical Agents Detected	TIMS Detected	Sensitivity	Resistance to Interferents	Response Time	Start-Up Time	Detection States	Alarm Capability	Portability	Battery Needs	Power Capabilities	Environment	Durability	Unit Cost	Operator Skills Training
7	GID-3, Chemical Agent Detection System Ion Mobility Spectrometry	●	◕	◔	●	◐	◔	●	◐	●	●	●	●	TBD	●	◐
56	CW Sentry Surface Acoustic Wave, Microsensor Systems, Inc.	●	◕	◔	◔	◔	◔	●	○	●	◕	◐	○	○	●	◐
61	ADLIF System/ Flame Photometry Military	●	○	◔	●	○	◔	●	○	●	◕	TBD	●	○	○	◐
66	Miran 981B Multipoint, Ambient Air Monitoring System, Infrared Spectroscopy	○	TBD	◔	◕	TBD	◐	●	○	TBD	TBD	TBD	TBD	TBD	●	TBD
67	Automatic Continuous Environmental Monitor (ACEM) 900 GC	●	○	◕	○	○	◐	○	○	NA	○	●	○	○	○	○
105	Model TS400 Toxic Gas Detector Electrochemistry	○	◕	◕	◔	○	◐	○	○	●	◕	●	●	◔	●	◐
151	Fixed Site/Remote Chemical Agent Detector, Ion Mobility Spectrometry	●	○	TBD	TBD	TBD	TBD	◕	○	TBD	TBD	TBD	TBD	TBD	◐	●
158	GID-2A Chemical Detector	●	◕	◕	●	◐	◔	●	◔	NA	○	◐	●	○	●	◐

'NA' - the specific selection factor is not applicable for the piece of equipment.
'TBD' (to be determined) - there is currently no data available to support that selection factor.

52

Table 5-11. Fixed-Site Analytical Laboratory Systems
May 2000

ID #	Detector Name	Chemical Agents Detected	TIMS Detected	Sensitivity	Resistance to Interferents	Response Time	Start-Up Time	Detection States	Alarm Capability	Portability	Battery Needs	Power Capabilities	Environment	Durability	Unit Cost	Operator Skills	Training
31	Miniature Chemical Agent Monitor (MINICAM)	●	○	◕	◔	TBD	◕	●	◔	NA	○	TBD	TBD	○	○	○	
33	Miniature Air Sampling System (MASS)	●	◑	NA	NA	NA	◑	TBD	◔	◕	●	TBD	TBD	TBD	○	○	
44	Kodiak 1200 Mass Spectrometry	●	TBD	TBD	◕	◔	●	●	○	NA	○	◐	TBD	○	◐	○	
45	API 365 Mass Spectrometry (Pe Sciex)	●	TBD	TBD	●	◔	●	TBD	○	NA	○	TBD	TBD	○	◑	◑	
46	Agilent 6890-5973, GC/MSD	●	TBD	●	○	○	●	●	○	NA	○	○	●	○	○	○	
47	HP 6890 GC/Flame Photometry	●	TBD	TBD	○	○	◑	◕	○	NA	○	◐	TBD	○	○	○	
48	Automatic Continuous Air Monitoring System (ACAMS) GC/Flame Photometry	●	○	◕	◔	○	◑	●	○	NA	○	TBD	●	○	○	○	
49	Dual-Flame Photometric Detector GC/Flame Photometry	○	TBD	TBD	○	◔	●	●	○	NA	○	TBD	TBD	TBD	○	○	

'NA' - the specific selection factor is not applicable for the piece of equipment.
'TBD' (to be determined) - there is currently no data available to support that selection factor.
See Table 5-13 for selection factor definitions.

53

Table 5-11. Fixed-Site Analytical Laboratory Systems
May 2000

ID #	Detector Name	Chemical Agents Detected	TIMs Detected	Sensitivity	Resistance to Interferents	Response Time	Start-Up Time	Detection States	Alarm Capability	Portability	Battery Needs	Power Capabilities	Environment	Durability	Unit Cost	Operator Skills	Training
52	Saturn 2000 GC with Mass Spectrometry	●	TBD	TBD	◕	○	●	TBD	○	NA	○	TBD	TBD	○	○	○	
53	HP 2350 Atomic Emission Detector Gas Chromatography with Mass Spectrometry	●	TBD	TBD	TBD	○	●	●	○	NA	○	TBD	TBD	○	○	○	
54	Infrared Detector for Gas Chromatograph	●	TBD	TBD	●	TBD	●	◐	○	NA	○	TBD	TBD	○	○	○	
71	Viking 573 GC with Mass Spectrometry	●	◕	●	●	○	◕	TBD	○	●	●	◐	●	○	○	○	
72	Trace Ultra High Sensitivity GC with FTIR	●	TBD	◕	TBD	◔	●	TBD	TBD	NA	○	○	TBD	TBD	○	○	
73	Innova Gas Analyzer Type 1301 Photoacoustic Infrared Spectroscopy	●	TBD	◕	●	◔	◕	◐	○	●	●	◐	TBD	○	◐	◐	
86	Hewlett Packard HP1000 HPLC System	TBD	TBD	TBD	TBD	TBD	TBD	●	TBD	TBD	TBD	TBD	TBD	TBD	TBD	TBD	
87	Perkin-Elmer Turbo LC Plus HPLC System	TBD	TBD	TBD	TBD	TBD	TBD	TBD	TBD	TBD	TBD	TBD	TBD	TBD	TBD	TBD	

'NA' - the specific selection factor is not applicable for the piece of equipment.
'TBD' (to be determined) - there is currently no data available to support that selection factor.

Table 5-11. Fixed-Site Analytical Laboratory Systems
May 2000

ID #	Detector Name	Chemical Agents Detected	TIMs Detected	Sensitivity	Resistance to Interferents	Response Time	Start-Up Time	Detection States	Alarm Capability	Portability	Battery Needs	Power Capabilities	Environment	Durability	Unit Cost	Operator Skills	Training
88	Shimadzu LC-10 HPLC System	TBD	TBD	TBD	TBD	TBD	TBD	TBD	TBD	TBD	TBD	TBD	TBD	TBD	TBD	TBD	TBD
89	Varian ProStar Analytical HPLC System	TBD	TBD	TBD	TBD	TBD	TBD	TBD	TBD	TBD	TBD	TBD	TBD	TBD	TBD	TBD	TBD
90	Dionex DX-500 IC System (Ion Chromatography)	TBD	TBD	TBD	TBD	TBD	TBD	TBD	TBD	TBD	TBD	TBD	TBD	TBD	TBD	TBD	TBD
91	Brinkmann Metrohm Model 1761 IC System	TBD	TBD	TBD	TBD	TBD	TBD	◕	TBD	TBD	TBD	TBD	TBD	TBD	TBD	TBD	TBD
92	Hewlett-Packard HP3D CZE System (Capillary Zone Electrophoresis)	TBD	TBD	TBD	TBD	TBD	TBD	◕	TBD	TBD	TBD	TBD	TBD	TBD	TBD	TBD	TBD
93	Beckman-Coulter P/ACE 5000 CZE System	TBD	TBD	TBD	TBD	TBD	TBD	●	TBD	TBD	TBD	TBD	TBD	TBD	TBD	TBD	TBD
94	Bio-Rad BioFocus 2000 System CZE	TBD	TBD	TBD	TBD	TBD	TBD	TBD	TBD	TBD	TBD	TBD	TBD	TBD	TBD	TBD	TBD

'NA' - the specific selection factor is not applicable for the piece of equipment.
'TBD' (to be determined) - there is currently no data available to support that selection factor.
See Table 5-13 for selection factor definitions.

Table 5-12. Stand-Off Detection Systems
May 2000

ID #	Detector Name	Chemical Agents Detected	TIMs Detected	Sensitivity	Resistance to Interferents	Response Time	Start-Up Time	Detection States	Alarm Capability	Portability	Battery Needs	Power Capabilities	Environment	Durability	Unit Cost	Operator Skills	Training
40	M21 Automatic Chemical Agent Alarm/ FTIR (Remote Standoff CA Alarm and Sensor)	●	○	○	◔	◔	◐	●	○	TBD	TBD	●	●	TBD	TBD	◐	◐
41	AN/KAS-1/AN/KAS-1A Chemical Warfare Directional Detector Infrared Spectroscopy	◔	○	TBD	◔	◔	◐	◐	◔	NA	○	◐	●	TBD	TBD	◐	◐
42	Air Sentry-FTIR Infrared Spectroscopy	●	○	TBD	◔	●	◔	TBD	○	NA	○	TBD	TBD	○	○	○	○
43	Laser Remote Detector (LIDAR) Military	◔	○	○	◔	◔	◐	●	○	TBD	●	TBD	TBD	○	○	○	○

'NA' - the specific selection factor is not applicable for the piece of equipment.
'TBD' (to be determined) - there is currently no data available to support that selection factor.
See Table 5-13 for selection factor definitions.

Table 5-13. Selection Factor Key For Chemical Detection Equipment
May 2000

Symbol	Chemical Agents Detected	TIMs Detected	Sensitivity	Resistance to Interferents	Response Time	Start-Up Time	Detection States	Alarm Capability	Portability	Battery Needs	Power Capabilities	Environment	Durability	Unit Cost	Operator Skills	Training
●	Detects all of the nerve and blister agents	Detects all of the TIMs listed	Detects at one-tenth IDLH for all detectable chemicals	Responds only to chemical agents and TIMs	Less than 10 seconds	Less than 30 seconds	Detects chemicals in all three states	Audible and Visible alarm	Less than 2 pounds and handheld	Operates on standard, inexpensive, and readily available batteries for eight hours of continuous use	Battery or AC Powered	Operates in all expected environments	Able to operate with rough handling	Less than $500 per unit	No special skills or training required	No special training required
◕	Detects either the nerve or blister agent class	Detects multiple TIMs	Detects at IDLH for all detectable chemicals	Has a few non-critical interferants	Between 10 and 60 seconds	Between 30 and 60 seconds	Detects chemicals in two states	Audible alarm only	Between 2 and 5 pounds and handheld		Battery Powered			Between $500 and $2000 per unit		
◑		Detects one TIM	Detects at IDLH for one or more detectable chemicals	Has many interferants		Between 1 and 5 minutes	Detects chemicals in one state	Visible alarm only	Between 5 and 10 pounds	Operates on standard, inexpensive, and readily available batteries for two hours of continuous use		Operates in most environments	Able to operate after being moved but not after rough handling	Between $2000 and $5000 per unit	No special skills but training required	Less than 8 hours training required
◔					Between 60 seconds and 2 minutes	Between 5 and 30 minutes			Between 10 and 50 pounds		Vehicle or AC Powered					
○	Detects none of the nerve or blister agents	Detects none of the TIMs listed	Does not detect IDLH levels	Does not discriminate between chemical agents/TIMs and interferants	Greater than 2 minutes	More than 30 minutes	No capability	No capability	Greater than 50 pounds	Operates on special order and expensive batteries	AC Powered	Operation is restricted to certain environments	Must remain stationary	More than $5000 per unit	Technician required to operate equipment	More than 8 hours training required

The gray cells designate that the symbol is not applicable for the selection factor.

APPENDIX A
RECOMMENDED QUESTIONS ON DETECTORS

Recommended Questions on Detectors

Buying detection, protection, and decontamination equipment to respond to the threatened terrorist use of chemical or biological warfare agents may be new for Public Safety Agencies. To help procurement officials obtain the best value for their domestic preparedness dollar, the staff of the Center for Domestic Preparedness (Fort McClellan, AL), Military Chemical/Biological Units, the National Institute of Justice, and members of a federal Interagency Board (that includes representatives from the state and local law enforcement, medical, and fire communities) have compiled a series of questions. These questions should assist officials in selecting products from the large number in the present day marketplace. Requesting vendors to provide written responses to your specific questions may also be helpful in the decision process.

1. What agents has the equipment been tested against?
2. Who conducted the tests? Have the test results been verified by an independent laboratory or only by the manufacturer? What were the results of those tests?
3. What common substances cause a 'false positive' reading or interference?
4. Is the test data available? Where?
5. What types of tests were conducted? Have any engineering changes or manufacturing process changes been implemented since the testing? If so, what were the changes?
6. Can the equipment detect both large and small agent concentrations?
7. Are there audible and visual alarms? What are their set points and how hard is it to change them? Are the alarm set points easily set to regulatory or physiologically significant values?
8. How quickly does the detector respond to a spike in the agent concentration? How quickly does the detector clear when taken to a clean area? What is the response time of the detector to a spike in the agent? How much time does the detector take to clear when taken to a clean area?
9. How long does it take to put the equipment into operation? Can it be efficiently operated by someone in a Level A suit?
10. How long do the batteries last? How long does it take to replace batteries or recharge? What is the cost of new batteries? Are the expended batteries HAZMAT and what is the cost of disposal of batteries?
11. How long has the company/manufacturer been involved with the Chem-Bio-Nuc and first responder industries? You may also ask for references.
12. Is the company currently supplying its product(s) to similar agencies? If so, who? Ask for names and phone numbers of departments currently using the company's equipment. Ask to follow-up on the phone any written testimonials.
13. What additional items are required to operate/maintain the equipment? At what cost? What training materials are provided – manuals, videotapes, CD ROMs? What is the cost of training materials?
14. What type of warranty/maintenance support is offered? Cost?
15. What is the return rate on the equipment under warranty? What are the top five reasons for failure?
16. What are the required on-hand logistical support and costs? How often does the equipment need to be sent back to the manufacturer for maintenance?
17. How often does the equipment require calibration? Does calibration require returning the equipment to the manufacturer? Does the calibration involve hazardous materials?
18. What special licenses/permits/registrations are required to own/operate the equipment?
19. What similar companies' products has this product been tested against? What were the results of the tests? Compare it in cost and performance to M-8/M-9 paper.
20. What is the shelf life of the equipment? (open exposed, open unexposed, closed exposed, closed unexposed)

21. What is required to decontaminate the equipment if taken into the Hot Zone?
22. What capability does this equipment give me that I do not currently possess? What equipment can I do away with if I purchase this? Is it only used for military chemicals?
23. Does this equipment require any hazardous materials for cleaning? If yes, what are they?
24. Taking weight and size into consideration, what procedures/process are needed to employ down range? How hard is it to decontaminate to get it out of the Hot Zone? What procedures/process are employed to decontaminate to remove from Hot Zone?
25. What is the theory of operation? Surface acoustic wave (SAW) photo ionization, flame ionization, etc.
26. What are the environmental limitations – high temperature, low temperature, humidity, sand/dust?
27. What are the storage requirements? (i.e., refrigerators, cool room, or no special requirements)
28. What training is required to use the equipment and interpret the results? Does the company provide this training, and what is the cost? How often is refresher training required?

Chemical/Biological Equipment Questions for Procurement Officials in Public Safety Agencies.

APPENDIX B
REFERENCES

REFERENCES

1. Bowen, Gregory W; *Chemical Warfare (CW)/ Biological Warfare (BW) Agent Sensor Technology Survey*, Battelle Memorial Institute, Columbus, OH, AD-B172264, January 29, 1993.

2. Brletich, Nancy; Waters, Mary Jo; Bowen, Gregory; Tracy, Mary Frances; *Worldwide Chemical Detection Equipment Handbook*, Chemical Warfare/Chemical and Biological Defense Information Analysis Center, Aberdeen Proving Ground, MD, AD-D754461, ISBN 1-888727-00-4, October 1995.

3. Longworth, Terri L; Cajigas, Juan C; Barnhouse, Jacob L; Ong, Kwok Y; Procell, Suzanne A; *Testing of Commercially Available Detectors Against Chemical Warfare Agents: Summary Report*, Edgewood Chemical Biological Center, Aberdeen Proving Ground, MD, AD-A364123, ECBC-TR-033, February 1999.

4. Stuempfle, A.K.; Howells, D.J.; Armour, S.J.; Boulet, C.A.; *International Task Force 25*: *Hazard From Industrial Chemicals Final Report*, Edgewood Research Development and Engineering Center, Aberdeen Proving Ground, MD, AD-B236562, ERDEC-SP-061, April 1998.

5. Widder, Jeffrey (PhD); Janus, Michael; Golly, Scott; Ewing, Kenneth (PhD); Barrett, John; *CSEPP Chemical Detection Equipment Assessment Volume I*, July 1998.

6. Widder, Jeffrey (PhD); Janus, Michael; Golly, Scott; Ewing, Kenneth (PhD), Barrett, John; *CSEPP Chemical Detection Equipment Assessment Volume II*, July 1998.

7. Widder, Jeffrey (PhD); Saubier, Leo; Janus, Michael; Jackson, William; Golly, Scott; *Final Report on Chemical Detection Equipment Market Survey for Emergency Responders*, September 23, 1998.

8. *Potential Military Chemical/Biological Agents and Compounds,* FM 3-9, AFR 355-7; NAVFAC P-467, Army Chemical School, Fort, McClellan, AL, December 12, 1990.

U.S. Department of Justice
Office of Justice Programs
810 Seventh Street N.W.
Washington, DC 20531

Janet Reno
Attorney General

Daniel Marcus
Acting Associate Attorney General

Mary Lou Leary
Acting Assistant Attorney General

Julie E. Samuels
Acting Director, National Institute of Justice

For grant and funding information, contact:
Department of Justice Response Center
800-421-6770

Office of Justice Programs
World Wide Web Site:
http://www.ojp.usdoj.gov

National Institute of Justice
World Wide Web Site:
http://www.ojp.usdoj.gov/nij